P9-CDK-109

ReVisions

ReVisions

Seeing Torah Through a Feminist Lens

Rabbi Elyse Goldstein

Jewish Lights Publishing
Woodstock, Vermont

This edition published in 1998 in the United States by Jewish Lights Publishing
A Division of LongHill Partners, Inc.
Sunset Farm Offices, Route 4
P.O. Box 237
Woodstock, VT 05091
Tel: (802) 457-4000
Fax: (802) 457-4004
www.jewishlights.com

Library of Congress Cataloging in Publication Data

Goldstein, Elyse.
Revisions : seeing Torah through a feminist lens / Elyse Goldstein.
p. cm.
"Key Porter books."
Includes bibliographical references and index.
ISBN 1-58023-047-4 (hardcover)
1. Women in the Bible. 2. Bible. O.T.-Feminist criticism. 3. Purity, Ritual-Biblical teaching.
4. Feminism-Religious aspects-Judaism. 5. Women in Judaism. I. Title.
BS1199.W7G67 1998
221.6'082-dc21 98-36894
CIP

Printed in Canada in 1998 by Key Porter Books Limited.
Design: Peter Maher
Electronic formatting: Heidi Palfrey

Printed and bound in Canada

98 99 00 01 6 5 4 3 2 1

The author gratefully acknowledges permission to reprint from the following:

"We All Stood Together" and "Meditation on Menstruation" by Merle Feld have appeared in a number of anthologies. They will appear in *A Spirited Life*, a memoir in poetry and prose by Merle Feld (SUNY Press). Used with permission of Merle Feld.

"A Meditation on the Feminine Nature of Shekhinah" from *She Who Dwells Within* by Lynn Gottlieb. Copyright © 1995 by Lynn Gottlieb. Reprinted by permission of HarperCollins Publishers Inc.

Excerpt from "Saint Francis and the Sow" from *Three Books*. Copyright © 1993 by Galway Kinnell. Previously published in *Mortal Acts, Mortal Worlds* (1990). Reprinted by permission of Houghton Mifflin Company. All rights reserved.

"Born of Water" from *Poems "To Life!" Sung Series* (as yet unpublished) by Sarah Louise Giroux. Copyright © 1997 by Sarah Louise Giroux. Reprinted by permission.

From *Woman's Mysteries* by M. Esther Harding. © 1987 by the C.G. Jung Foundation for Analytical Psychology. Reprinted by arrangement with Shambhala Publications, Inc., 300 Massachusetts Ave., Boston, MA 02115.

Contents

To my mother, Terry, who could and should have been
a rabbi, had the doors been open in her day;
who never laughed at her daughter's dream of being a rabbi

To my sister, Marsha ז"ל, may her memory be a blessing,
who taught me to take it easy and laugh a little
at the world I take so seriously

Acknowledgments

This book began on a kitchen table—that place which is so much the heart and the pulse of what goes on in women's lives. Over a cup of coffee, in between children's needs being met, while dinner is cooking, we dream and discuss.

I was sitting at a very cluttered kitchen table with author Michele Landsberg one day, planning for the yearly feminist Succot celebration that takes place in Toronto. Michele and I collaborated on that program for several years, and we met in her kitchen to work and to shmooze. It was in one of those magical women's moments, while making tea and talking about our kids, that I opened my heart to her. "Michele," I said, "I'm turning forty this year, and there are three things I need to do to face my midlife with courage. I need to move from our crowded house in an ultra-religious neighborhood where my kids are shunned. I need to have a daughter. (I have three sons—a feminist challenge worth a book in itself!) And I need to share my feminist vision of Torah with more people outside of my students here in Toronto. It is a vision I think is inclusionary and open and will bring more people to see the Torah more creatively. That's what I need to do."

"Elyse," she answered, "I can't help you move. I don't think you'll have a daughter. But I can help you with your third challenge. Write your book and share your vision." I thank Michele with deep appreciation for seeing the book more clearly than I did at first. She arranged my first meeting with publishers, and guided me through many an anxious morning of writing. And she was right. I didn't have a daughter, at least not physically. In a sense, this book is my daughter.

This book is also my sons. It has their indelible touch upon it. I see raising the next generation of feminist men as holy work. For my sons, Noam, Carmi and Micah, I hope that books such as this will one day be required curriculum. I pray the feminist vision of Torah will soon be the normative one. I dream that, when you are adults, you will live in a world where women's voices and women's interpretations of sacred texts are standard and plentiful.

Many wonderful people put valuable time and effort into seeing this book become a reality. I would like to thank Malcolm Lester and Kathy Lowinger, who first shared my enthusiasm and guided me as a new author; my editor, Barbara Berson, for her sharp focus, keen skills, and her ability to "revision" this book; Susan Renouf at Key Porter Books for her calming optimism; and Sarah Swartz, whose accurate, thoughtful, challenging and loving insights beautifully shaped the book in its final stages. Several friends and teachers read the manuscript and were very helpful yet kind in their critique. Thank you to Amy Dattner, Rabbi Dayle Friedman and Rabbi Michael Strassfeld. I am honored that Rabbi W. Gunther Plaut, one of the great scholars of our time and a personal mentor of mine, also read the manuscript and gave advice.

When Rabbi Irving Greenberg graciously consented to write the foreword for this book, I was overjoyed. He has been my hero for many years. He is a truly magnificent author and teacher, who as an Orthodox yet pluralistic rabbi remains a sensitive supporter and critic, when necessary, of the Jewish feminist movement. His involvement enriches this book immeasurably.

For the past fifteen years as a rabbi, my greatest joy has been in teaching. I see my teaching as a tool for helping people reevaluate, and thus revalue Jewish tradition. When my listeners shine with a new understanding of a text they initially saw as irrelevant or obsolete, or when they feel included in the text in a personal way, or when they recognize themselves as a link in the ancient chain of Judaism, because of a word, a phrase, a nuance I have introduced, I feel blessed.

It says in the Talmud, tractate Taanit 7a: "Rabbi Hanina said, 'I have learned much from my teachers, and even more from my colleagues, but most of all I have learned from my students.'" How true that is. This book is possible only because of my students, whose provocative questions through the years form the basis of these chapters. I am especially grateful to my first students at Temple Beth Or of the Deaf in New York, who challenged me to enter their language, their culture and their way of being Jewish. They taught me what it means to rise above being marginal. I appreciate those who trained me and sat through my first classes at Holy Blossom Temple in Toronto when I was their "young assistant." I lovingly acknowledge my congregants at Temple Beth David of the South Shore in Canton, Massachusetts, who always came loyally to adult education classes and took Torah, and my "revisions," seriously.

It is to my past and present students at Kolel: A Centre for Liberal Jewish Learning in Toronto that I owe the deepest thanks. Kolel has become a laboratory for new ideas, both mine and theirs. Much of the wisdom I have gained from Kolel students, especially those in the "Women in Judaism," "Women in Torah," "Women in Tanach" and "Feminist Theology" classes, has found its way into these chapters.

And, of course, I give thanks to the Holy One for opening my eyes, guiding my steps, sustaining me and bringing me to this project.

On Friday evenings, before Shabbat, Jews traditionally sing a love-song to welcome the Sabbath queen. The song is called "Lecha Dodi," which means "Come, my beloved." One of the verses ends with these words: *Sof ma'ase b'machshavah techilla*, which means "though done last it is first in thought." Throughout the writing of this book, I have thought of how blessed I am to have a loving partner. I mention him last though he is first in thought. My beloved husband, my *ezer k'negdi*, helper, critic, friend and soulmate, Baruch Browns-Sienna, is truly, vitally, and in holy ways my other half, as it was in the days of Eden.

(P.S. We bought a new house last year. And I'm surviving my midlife crisis—so far.)

SHEVAT 5758, JANUARY 1998

Foreword

by Rabbi Irving (Yitz) Greenberg

ReVisions is an important contribution to the process of making the learning of Torah central to Jewish life today. (When learning Torah and applying its lessons to living is at the heart of the Jewish community, then the continuity crisis will be over and the Jewish renaissance will have begun.) This book will inspire liberal religious Jews by showing how much they can learn from tradition and how much they can contribute to it. It will inspire traditional religious Jews by showing them how fascinating and full of unexpected twists and turns the process of learning Torah is.

Rabbi Elyse Goldstein's *ReVisions* offers us a cogent feminist interpretation of key scriptural narratives and a stimulating revisioning of a key ritual complex (purity/impurity and the symbolic roles of blood and water). The book's last section is a thought-provoking, sensitive and balanced treatment of a critical theological challenge: must we re-open to the goddess image in order to save the understanding of God from sexual anthropomorphism? Is there any other way to enable our metaphors/image of God to sustain women's full and equal dignity?

Let me confess that I hesitated to write this foreword. In general, forewords are a continuation of the traditional *haskama* [approbation/validation] of a book in which the supposedly senior, established, "authoritative" person vouches for the importance of the author and the bona fides of the book. "What is the point?" I asked myself. In liberal circles, a validation by an Orthodox rabbi will not do much for the book (and may be used by more radical feminists as "proof" that Elyse Goldstein sold out). In traditional circles, much of the material will not be appreciated (and may be used by more radical fundamentalists as "proof" that Yitz Greenberg sold out).

Nevertheless, I determined to write these words for three primary reasons. One is my long-standing admiration for Rabbi Elyse Goldstein. She represents the best impulses in Reform Judaism—the desire to profoundly connect to Torah, to deepen study, to reappropriate observance, to continuously hold a respectful dialogue with traditional Jews even in disagreement, and despite conflicts in world views.

I am an Orthodox pluralist who believes that overarching principles unite the denominations despite the fundamental disagreements between us. These common principles legitimate Reform (and other liberal religious movements) as covenantal partners not only when they are right, but even when they are wrong in belief and practice. However, pluralism should mean more than legitimating the other; it entails allowing for mutual partnership. In this model, each side has a stake in the other. Since the Other can reach Jews that I cannot, then anything I can do to strengthen the Other is a *mitzvah*. I want to strengthen Elyse Goldstein and the best in Reform, so that the movement can raise the level and seriousness of its people and thereby raise the level of all Jews.

The second motivation for my involvement is my belief that every generation must write its commentaries on Torah. This fulfills Rashi's understanding of *shma*—that through learning we come to experience the commandments/words of Torah as being of "today." Then they will not be viewed by us as some ancient royal decree received in writing; i.e., we avoid the danger that Torah may be authoritative but not relevant. (See Rashi on Deuteronomy 6, v. 4–7, especially v. 6.)

This book of commentary is written from the feminist perspective. Feminism is the movement that seeks to realize the Torah's dream of every human being in the image of God. On the basis of the Talmud (Sanhedrin 37A) I understand this to mean that every human has the intrinsic dignities of infinite value, equality and uniqueness. I share Elyse Goldstein's conviction that in the first chapter of Genesis—which is *the* biblical Creation account—these degrees of dignity are bestowed on men and women alike. In my reading, Chapter 1 describes the world that God intends to create, a world which some day will be fully realized. Genesis in Chapters 2–4 shows that this is not the world that we live in—now. We live in a world that is cursed. The curse expresses itself in many ways: in the hard labor and struggle to wrest a living which leaves many in poverty and leads others to be grasping and exploitative in their affluence; in the inequality of men and women in which typically men rule but all humans suffer from the distortion in that process; in the war of humans against animals, against nature, against each other.

The Jewish people comes into being to show the way to restore blessing to the world. Its mission is to pioneer on the frontier, working toward a perfected earth in which the original, intended abundance, equality and harmony will be established. Therefore, when the final history will be written, feminism (whatever its excesses or errors) will be judged to be a force for Divine blessing and realization of the Torah's vision.

In order to play this role successfully, feminism must come to grips with the tradition even as the tradition must reckon with feminism. In this book, Rabbi Goldstein shows that, for feminists, the choice is between rejection, reinvention and revision of the tradition. Here again, I believe that her judgement will be proven right. Invention can help, but it cannot do as much to bring the past with us into the future. Rejection pays too high a price in loss of the past; it entails leaving behind divine treasures and a sense of continuity. Revision from within is the key. It is not so important that I, as an Orthodox Jew, will differ on many specific points with this book. The bottom line is that the method of revision is needed to achieve vitality for Orthodox Jews as well as for liberal Jews. On the details, we will argue—and that too generates vitality.

This brings me to the third reason for writing this foreword. It is best summed up in a favorite midrash that my father, Rabbi Eliyahu Chayim Greenberg, *zichrono livracha* would often cite when seeking to learn with his adolescent son. In a most obscure passage in Numbers 21:15, it says: "Therefore, the Book of the Wars of the Lord speaks of . . . Wahev in Sufah and the wadis: the Arnon . . ." In a wonderful pun, the Gemara comments: when it comes to the Wars of the Lord, then it is simply *wa-hev b'Sufah*. A father and son, or a teacher and student who learn Torah together, even if they become enemies one to another will not leave that place without becoming loving of one another. For Scripture states *wa-hev b'sufah*, and in this case read it not *wa-hev* but *a-hev*, e.g., a lover; also read it not *b'Sufah* but *b'Sofah*, i.e., in the end. [Kiddushin 31B] My father believed that out of the struggle to learn and interpret Torah texts, people become attached to the Torah—and each other. It made no difference if the disagreements were fierce with no-holds-barred. Even if the protagonists were in conflict and this led to anger and enmity—if the connections to Torah were kept, then the human connections would be reborn at an even higher level.

At a time when relations between the denominations have become poisoned, we must reassert the unifying power of Torah. When rhetoric between Orthodox Jews and liberal religious Jews has deteriorated into angry insults and mud slinging, then we must restore dialogue by "talking in Torah" and by arguing over its proper interpretation.

This book draws me—as I believe it will attract many others—because in it a Reform/liberal teacher engages traditional Jews (indeed, all Jews) by offering alternative interpretations of Torah. Many insights stand out. To cite just a few: bonding as biblical women's method compared to conflict among the males; the internal dialogues between male and female aspects of divinity; her interpretation of the snake; her portrait of the strong women of the Exodus; her exploration of the religious significance of menstruation, including the brilliant suggestion that "if blood seals covenant, then women's blood seals our covenant, at puberty and through a natural flow rather than a human cut"; the twin potential in all potent symbols, including birth and decay, purity and impurity; her exploration of *brit milah* as the ritual moment "where men birth through blood, when they connect physically as women do"; her extraordinary treatment of God-language. All these passages cannot be summarized adequately, but must be read.

Many Orthodox Jews will reject aspects of Goldstein's terminology such as "taboo" or "patriarchal," which are so freely used in this book. But Rabbi Goldstein makes clear that she does not use these words dismissively. She argues respectfully; she learns from the tradition and seeks to embrace where she can.

In this book, traditional Jews will meet a liberal Judaism which cannot be written off as assimilationist. It cannot be judged as looking to take on less of the tradition because it is lazy or is excessively under the spell of the West. Thus traditional Jews may learn from or even be inspired by its new understandings of Torah. Even where they disagree, they may be sensitized to issues in the tradition that need to be worked on and revisioned.

However, even if traditional Jews are not educated or upgraded by this book, it will still make an important contribution. At this moment, the Jewish community needs us to grasp each other's hand and sit down to study together. We need to argue, to quarrel, to fiercely criticize each other's mastery and use of Torah. Let the argument between Liberal and Orthodox Jews turn on interpreting verses or applying *halachic* models, on how to draw behavioral conclusions from fundamental principles, on how best to integrate rituals into a frame of meaning.

This book invites us to put aside demeaning rhetoric and dismissive stereotypes and learn Torah together. This book enables us to leave behind insulting conceptions of each other and to wrestle with our understandings of God and the impact of God-language on people. Can you imagine a community-wide, perhaps a world-wide network of *batei midrash* [study halls] in which Jews of every stripe learn, analyze, argue, engage passionately? Can anyone doubt that in such circumstance, the Torah has the power to elicit the capacity for love which is latent in every individual?

When the whole Jewish world is a cauldron cooking with learning and dialogue over Torah, then we will see the fulfillment of the Talmudic promise that "they will not leave that place without becoming loving of one another." When that day comes, this book, *ReVisions*, will be honored. In the meantime, go and study it.

. . . for everything flowers, from within, of self blessing;
though sometimes it is necessary
to reteach a thing its loveliness . . .

Galway Kinnel, "St. Francis and the Sow"

Introduction

I am a rabbi. I am a woman. I am a feminist. To be perfectly honest, sometimes reading the Torah terrifies me. How can one book speak so powerfully to my Jewish soul while at the same time disturbing so painfully my female soul? I know I am not the only one who lives in these two worlds. I admit that I love the Torah, even with all its androcentricity—men at the center, women on the outside. I'm drawn to its barren, strong and loving mothers, and its silent, powerful fathers. I need the Ten Commandments, and the shaking, quaking mountain of Sinai, and all the laws of kindness to strangers, orphans and animals. When I read the Torah, I feel as if I am standing in both the past and the present, and I am keenly aware that I am also part of the future. This book has been the record of my tribe, my clan, my people's way of trying to speak to and about the Divine, for thousands of years. It is mine, more than Shakespeare or fifteenth-century French poetry or any great literature is truly mine. It is my family's spiritual diary, even if I do not like all the entries.

Since it is mine, since I am one of those Jews who feels ownership of Jewish sacred text, I also feel called to critique it. Since it is mine, I have the duty to help it make sense today as more than a stale and dusty relic from my family's attic. Mine is not a judgement from the outside, based on a sketchy familiarity with old stories. It is a judgement from inside, from a lover.

Because I am a lover, I want to be among those who ministered at the Tabernacle. I want to feel what Aaron's wife felt when their two sons, Nadav and Avihu, were struck down at the altar for offering strange fire. I want to participate in the conversations between Sarah and Hagar. I want to know which ceremony Dinah was trying to get to when she "went out to see the daughters of the land." Like a lover, I want to be *inside*: inside the events, part of the circle with those who participate.

I also need to be among those who are shocked at Lot's offer of his unmarried daughters to placate the evil men of his town. I challenge why Lot's wife could not look back. I vindicate Eve for her role in bringing knowledge, not death, to the world.

I am painfully aware of how the Torah has been used to justify women's subordination, the despoilment of the earth, and slavery. But I also experience how the Torah has been used to fight for liberation, to end exploitation, and to underscore the inherent worth of every human being. That is why I feel called to both defend it and challenge it.

This defence and challenge happens to be a traditional Jewish exercise. The word "revise" means "to look over and correct; to review, alter or amend; a re-examination." Throughout the generations, rabbis and scholars have taken the text and manipulated it, interpreted it, reread it and retold it. These rabbis are the original revisionists, for they indeed reexamined and then altered, albeit within acceptable traditional limits. They used parables, stories and metaphors to explain away any seeming contradictions between verses, or passages they found perplexing and morally ambiguous. For example, in his interpretation of the Genesis story of the near-sacrifice of Isaac, the twelfth-century French commentator Rashi painted Abraham as a religious zealot who insisted on the sacrifice himself, even when God relented. Rashi was disturbed, as many modern readers are, by the idea that God would need or want such a sacrifice in the first place. He needed to know why, as modern readers do. He wanted to defend Abraham, while criticizing the subtext of abuse by a father.

I use the title *ReVisions* for this book because I want readers both to revise—in the classic dictionary definition of reexamine and alter—and to see the text anew, to have a new vision, a "revision," of Torah.

Some Torah stories speak of female metaphors: water and a well, barrenness and desert; poetic images that spark the imagination. A revision of those common Torah pictures as female pictures is a way to see Torah through a more feminine lens. Some Torah stories are graphically physical, delineating the pure and impure. A revision of the blood taboos suggests the power as well as the repression of female sexuality. A revision of circumcision alludes to the curtailing of male sexuality. If we are prepared to rethink the metaphorical meaning of the stories we have known from childhood, we will bring to the modern Jewish world a feminist message that includes women in a new way, and refuses to let the Torah be used as a weapon against us.

A practical example. Open up the Torah, the book of Genesis, and you are immediately struck by this contradiction: in the first chapter, man and woman are created together, formed from the dust of the ground, and placed in Eden as partners. God calls them both "human" and all is well. Yet only a chapter later, Adam is lonely. He is put to sleep, and wakes up with a strange new being by his side whom he names "woman." What happened to the first woman created together with man? Are these two creation stories trying to tell us something about the spiritual relationship of male and female? Traditional male commentators reply with everything from justification for the sociological status of women to pronouncements about the nature of womanhood. So there must be room for new answers, which will find their way into a contemporary "tradition." If we can find an ultimate equality between men and women at the very beginning of the Bible, and we use the classical methodology of manipulation, interpretation and metaphor to do so, then we can change the way religion uses text to justify the spiritual and temporal subordination of women.

"Is it good for the Jews?" some ask, whether about politics, film, art, literature, education. The same can be asked by feminists. "Is it good for women?" is the question that defines a feminist vision of the world. How does this institution, that class, this film, that person's views affect women? How are women treated, portrayed, dealt with in a particular situation? A Jewish feminist will ask those questions of every Jewish organization, institution and synagogue that she or he encounters; at every *bris*, Bar or Bat Mitzvah, wedding, Shabbat service, camp, adult education class, she or he will ask, "What does this mean for women? And why?"

Twenty years ago, the nascent Jewish feminist movement had many of the same concerns as the general feminist one, centering around women's desires for equal status and equal access. Jewish women wanted to have the same opportunities, responsibilities and access to resources as men. The principle seemed simple enough: that the biological differences between men and women should not be translated into social barriers. Although men and women differed biologically, they were essentially the same. Thus, both proponents *and* opponents of early "women's lib" defined equality as sameness.

Today's feminism—and Jewish feminism along with it—has entered a second phase. We question if it is possible to both *equalize* as women and *specialize* as women. We are no longer so completely convinced that women and men are essentially the same. Do we see and experience the world differently because we are women? I believe we do. Many feminists now think that being female so deeply influences our perceptions of ourselves that it colors the way we perceive the rest of life and everything around us.

This book is not an egalitarian view of the Torah, but rather a feminist view. For my purposes, egalitarianism is not enough. Egalitarianism does not yet balance the predominance of male images, male perspectives, male views of the world. Egalitarianism does not yet adequately address or redress centuries of male exclusivity. Egalitarianism does not insist upon women's voices *as women* being heard; women's perspectives *as women* being sought; women's experiences *as women* being recorded.

This book is definitely woman-centered. It begins with the notion that women see the text differently than men do, ask different questions and bring different answers. It looks at all the stories of the Torah as enmeshed within a patriarchal interpretation and culture, in which it is not clear whether women are classified as "real" members of the tribe. It assumes that the Torah sees women as part of the enterprise, but not as its center. Throughout this book, I deconstruct in order to reconstruct. I ask of the Torah, "How ennobling is this story for women? How are this character's actions reflective of respect for women?" I ask: "Is it good for women?"

This book is also a feminist commentary. For centuries, the voice of women as observers and interpreters of the text went unheard. The reason for the lack of female interpretation is obvious. Commentary was the realm of the male scholar, the learned man. It was closed to women. To be viewed as a serious scholar of the Bible, one must be versed in ancient languages and cultures, and finally, in this generation, brilliant feminist scholars have taken up serious Bible commentary in this way. But we also need homiletics—the methodology used for interpreting the text through story, parable, sermon, discourse and the like—that are feminist. We need fantasies and tales that lend a human face—indeed, a female face—to the sacred text. We need more than an intellectual understanding of the ancient Near East. We also need the modern "spin" on stories we learnt as children, stories that not only shaped Western civilization but also defined each of us as human. There are many good books about women and the Bible, and a multiplicity of new and excellent scholarly works on the Bible by women. These include, among other approaches, studies of the origins of texts and literary forms, research into parallels in the literature of other cultures of the ancient Near East, and narrative criticism. To understand a feminist view of Torah, and what that view can reveal, we need to take a serious look at those sources. The bibliography at the end of this book is one tool for such an examination.

This book is a Jewish commentary, in the classic sense. Imagine a *mikraot gedolot*—a large Hebrew book with columns of commentaries written all around the central text. Imagine that we are studying the story of the Garden of Eden, specifically the part about the punishment given to Eve. "Your desire shall be for your husband, and he shall rule over you."

Rashi, the aforementioned medieval Frenchman, argues a literal point. What does the text mean by "rule"? He thinks it means that the man, not the woman, will be the sexual initiator. Even though you, the woman, shall desire him sexually, you will have to wait until *he* desires *you*.

Ibn Ezra, a Spanish grammarian of the 1100s, is concerned about the meaning of "desire." He understands it to mean "your obedience" shall be for your husband, that is to say, *your* desire shall be whatever *his* desire is. The woman's desire for her husband will be so strong that she will wish to do everything he commands.

Nachmanides, also called Ramban, an early thirteenth-century commentator from Spain, disagrees with both. He says Rashi errs, because a woman's natural modesty would preclude her from initiating sex anyway, so she would not have to be commanded to be modest in that area. Ibn Ezra also errs, he says, because the Hebrew word used in the text for "desire" always indicates sexuality, and cannot be used to mean obedience. In his mind the correct interpretation is this: she will desire him even though the pain of childbirth and pregnancy is so severe it would normally deter an attraction. "Your desire shall be for your husband" even though after the pain of labor your rational mind would not desire anything leading to such an outcome.

So, men busy explicating the female situation fill the commentary page, all from their personal, male points of view. Their views of women's "nature" totally color their biblical interpretation. We may imagine a woman's voice in the discussion, but we have to fill in the words she would say. What view would she hold? How would she interpret the Hebrew word for "rule"? We can imagine that when she speaks, the other commentators will rethink their definitions of womanhood. This book is an attempt to hear that female voice.

Come with me inside Torah texts. For the purposes of this book, Torah is meant in its literal sense: the Five Books of Moses, which is the first section of the three-section Hebrew Bible. *Neviim* (Prophets) and *Ketuvim* (Writings) are the other two parts of the full Hebrew Bible. These three sections together are called in Hebrew the *Tanach*, an acronym for *Torah*, *Neviim* and *Ketuvim*. When I quote or make reference to a piece of text from either Prophets or Writings, I use the term "Hebrew Bible." Otherwise, we concentrate on the Torah. I provide the textual references from the Torah in English, using my own translation. I indicate where words might have double meanings or other nuances.

This book progresses in a fashion similar to the way Jewish feminist thought on the Torah has progressed over the past twenty years: from the concrete to the abstract, from the individual woman to Jewish women as a collective. We begin with singular women, specific characters in the Torah and their interaction with the society around them. We then explore women's physicality; how our bodies, our cycles and our reproduction both influence us and affect the way the world views us. We conclude with women's spirituality, asking how the overriding masculinity of our traditional images of God affects us and our spirituality as women.

In each of the parts that make up this book, I imagine women's voices on that traditional commentary page. In the first part, "Women in the Torah," I challenge the easy answers often given in response to the ambivalence many women feel about the Torah and its sections dealing with women. I dispute the all-or-nothing interpretation that women are either totally oppressed or completely exalted.

In the second part, "Blood and Water: The Stuff of Life," I tackle the biblical sections on menstruation. What do the ancient blood taboos say to us as modern women? Here again I battle the black and white: that the blood taboos are either reactions to the rejection and repulsion that men felt about menstruation, or they result from the awe and respect our ancestors felt for women and the power of procreation. And when I look at modern society's taboos around menstruation, I also ask if there is any way feminists can reappropriate both *niddah*—the traditional laws around menstruation—and *mikveh*, the immersion in a body of natural water after a woman's period.

In the third part, "God, Goddess, Gender and the Torah," I examine the Torah and mythology, uncovering some of the vestiges we find in it of ancient goddess-worship and our ancestors' attraction to such practices. Time and again the prophets protested, and threatened the Israelites with retribution for turning to idolatry, and the Torah could have simply expunged all references to the early cults, groves, sacred pillars and the like. It did not, and I wonder why. In our day, there is a growing interest and attraction to the "old ways." They seem, on the surface, to posit a new spirituality, a way for women, nature, the earth and nurturing to be revalued. Some theologians and Bible scholars suggest that "the new knowledge of our past now being reclaimed signals a way out of our alienation from one another and from nature."[1] We will have to see what that new knowledge can mean for Jewish women.

This book is not about *rewriting* the Torah. It is about *rereading* it. Just as we cannot rewrite *The Merchant of Venice* to sanitize Shylock, rewriting the Torah will not change millennia of misogyny. This book is revisionist in the sense that it reimagines, or, the term I prefer, it "revisions." We examine themes that weave in and out of the text, fill in the silent gaps, and search for the paradigms. You will want to have your own text handy for reference as you read through this book; it is intended as a kind of Bible home companion. It is written for the lay person who wants to delve into the text in an innovative way.

For the past fifteen years, I have been teaching Torah to adults, and I have witnessed the yearning of both men and women to read the old tales with new eyes. There are those who view the traditional writings with anger, who feel disenfranchised or disillusioned. They still hope for a way in. There are those who have studied the Torah for years and yet have never asked critical sociological, historical or spiritual questions. For the religious or secular reader, the Bible is a source of insight. I believe it can offer women's insight as well.

A variety of ways now exist to see the Torah through a feminist lens. I will not count among them the school of apologetics that claims oppression simply does not occur in the Torah, or there are no cases of women treated as second-class citizens, and no injustices to women in the halachic-legal system posited by the Torah. These apologists respond with justifications and rationales to every critique, and claim that if we just understood the Torah better, we would clearly see how wonderfully women are portrayed and how our original concerns are simply misbegotten. (There may be some instances, they admit, in which women *seem* to be depicted in a negative light, but these few instances can easily be "fixed" by traditional commentators.) Such apologists claim that the problem lies not in the text, but in the reader. The text is held to be essentially enlightened for women, with isolated cracks that can be mended through exegesis and the beauty of a traditional life. These commentaries are not systematic critiques or feminist reexaminations. Although some appropriate the term "feminist" they are essentially interested in converting both the complaint and the complainer.

The more methodical feminist works can be grouped into three categories, which I term *rejectionist*, *inventive* and *revisionist*.

The rejectionist school repudiates the Torah outright. The Torah, rejectionists say, cannot be salvaged. It offers no hope for women. In fact, it systematically denies them hope. It presents a picture of woman and womanhood that is completely "other." They say, "It never was, it never will be. Trying to find it, or inventing it, is a deception." Such women have either abandoned organized religion, remaining only culturally connected to their tradition; they have chosen goddess, neo-pagan and witch religions; or devoted themselves to scholarship wholly critical of the Torah. As Naomi Goldenberg has written,

> Although I admire the efforts of the reformers, I see them engaged in a hopeless effort... Many feminists recommend ignoring parts of the Torah, but still claim the book as a whole is God-given. It is hard to deny that an eventual consequence of criticizing the correctness of any sacred text or tradition is to question why that text or tradition should be considered a divine authority at all... In order to develop a theology of women's liberation, feminists have to leave... the Bible behind them.[2]

The inventive writers are midrashists. They reappropriate the rabbinic use of parable, story and metaphor, creating explications and interpretations called *midrash* in Hebrew. They look deeply into the biblical texts and, failing to find women's voices or women's experience, they *invent* it. They say, "Failing to find it in the text, we will place it in the text ourselves." Like the classical midrashists, they may wander far from the original. Like the traditional midrashists, they add characters, provide dialogue, change scenes and suggest substitute readings. Norma Rosen notes,

> As a writer of fiction I am struck by the way in which the midrashic writing of the rabbis resembles the creation of fiction, with one important exception: Midrash, unlike writer's revisions, comes *after* the final story version, the one already in the biblical canon... midrash can sometimes seem like alternate drafts of a Bible story.[3]

For example, a feminist inventive midrash suggests that, in Genesis, God gave the choice of childbearing to both men and women, asking men first to accept this gift and responsibility, but men rejected it.[4] Reading Sarah into the Akedah, supplying Rebecca's feelings at the well, naming Lot's wife—all of these are inventive and fill in the details of women's lives, women's thoughts, their hopes and dreams.

The third group, the revisionists, among whom I count myself, represents a large proportion of today's feminist Jewish writers. We believe that, with all its problems, the Torah is still, at its core, a powerful and even liberating document; that within the Torah there is evidence of women valued for their personhood, women as spiritual individuals and women as central players in Jewish history; that the Torah is not first and foremost about women as secondary, oppressed subcitizens. There may even be instances we can uncover of women fighting the system and rebelling against their own oppression. Such a reading would say, "It's there—we just have to find it! It was. It existed!" Mary Ann Tolbert has called this the "remnant standpoint." She says it is a

> conscious effort to retrieve texts overlooked or distorted by patriarchal hermeneutics . . . [It] focuses its attention on texts involving women characters and explores their functions without the patriarchal presumption of marginality . . . To find within the writings of a culture so thoroughly patriarchal *any* counter-cultural material witnesses to the theological vitality and the importance of that remnant.[5]

Revisionists truly *revision*. They view the text head-on and place women squarely inside it, even if the traditional commentators have placed us on the outside. Revisionists recognize patriarchy in the Torah, but invite us to read the Torah with nonpatriarchal eyes. They reject the layers of later sexism and male commentary that have covered over and, in some ways, negated the original text. By reading the stories of individual women characters, we will discover that women were portrayed in much the same way as men: with the same kinds of strengths and weaknesses, loves and loyalties, fears and foibles. The difference between the sexes is explained as part of an inherited social order.[6] An example of this school of thought is my revision of the creation story of Adam and Eve in Part One.

My commentary, in the form of this book, is mostly revisionist, though sometimes inventive. I do not denounce the whole Torah, although I recognize that it has been used for the sociological justification of women's oppression for millennia. I do not dismiss the Torah, although I recognize it is used to perpetuate a system of woman as subject and object, a spectator in a religious journey not her own. I critique the entire system, but I do not reject the system. Like so many other women, I still live within it.

For some readers, this book may not go far enough. It will not be radical enough. It does not disown the Torah, nor blame the Hebrew Torah for all of patriarchy. And for other readers, this book may go too far. It does not take for granted the divinity of the authorship of the Torah. It does not assume the sacredness of inherited traditions. And it does not sidestep the possibility that the Torah knew of Hebrew symbiosis with other cultures in which women played very different roles, cultures that had a different image of their god than the Hebrews had of theirs.

But in a sense all feminist commentaries are deeply radical, because they go to the root. They are radical because in employing biblical scholarship, in utilizing traditional commentary, in "playing by the rules," *we use the system to critique the system*. In the words of Mary Ann Tolbert, "To destroy the oppressive structure of society using the tools that structure itself supplies is a process of erosion . . . Numerous such incremental changes, like erosion, will eventually bring down the fortress."[7] We want to bring down the fortress of patriarchal ownership of the Torah with the tools of the Torah itself.

This book only skims the surface. Feminism has become the main challenge to Judaism over the past twenty years, a challenge of modernity no less mighty than emancipation from the ghettos in the nineteenth century. The Orthodox world no longer ignores the tremendous influence of feminism, as evinced not only by the growing number of books defending the "traditional" role of women in Judaism, but by the number of scholarly articles in Orthodox rabbinic journals dealing with questions ranging from the permissibility of women saying Kaddish, the mourner's prayer traditionally obligatory for male family members, to husbands attending the birth of their children in hospital rooms. There is now an annual Orthodox Jewish feminist conference in New York, with increasingly large numbers of attendees every year. Because we Jews mostly live in the secular world, and because modern Orthodox women commonly interact with secular feminism in the workplace and marketplace, there is no lack of interest in the intersection of feminism and Judaism, even in the Orthodox world.

Why did I write this book? In a sense, to create my own spiritual diary. I want to express my existential loneliness and share it. I have spent my whole adult life walking these two paths of Judaism and feminism at the same time, straddling fences and trying to bring the two worlds together. On the Jewish path I try to include my feminism, to let it sing, to let it guide me. On the feminist path I try to include my Judaism, to also let it sing, to let it guide me. It has not been easy. In segments of the Jewish world, feminism is still the bad "f" word, a threatening, anxiety-producing expression. Feminists are accused of being traitorous, selfish and egotistical women who want to "take over." In the feminist world, Jews and their Jewish concerns are often seen as insulated and parochial. We are accused of not thinking globally, of participating in and thus perpetuating religious sexism which in turn has its own set of political repercussions.

I often feel alone in both of these worlds. My personal faith journey has taken me from left-wing college politics to a yeshivah in Jerusalem, complete with long-sleeved dresses and prayers three times a day, and then to the Reform rabbinical seminary. Through the rabbinate, I have met many others, both men and women, who are also trying to walk the two paths without losing their balance. I hope this book will help those straddling like me.

I wrote this book because I have been a rabbi for fifteen years, but a woman all of my life. I have been marginalized as a Jew, marginalized as a woman, doubly marginalized as a woman-Jew. I know what it means to be "other." I did not grow up with female rabbis as role models. I did not grow up with books like this one and the plethora of other worthy feminist Jewish books. Most of my mentors were men and I saw the Torah through their male lenses. I want other women to have what I did not.

And I wrote this book because I love the Torah, but I simply hate its sexism. I love the beauty of the Torah, its poetry, its literary devices, its surprise endings, the way the Hebrew language flows. I love its inherent ethical quality; its demands for justice and compassion; its unflinching support of the underdog; its values of family, fidelity, honesty and service. I hate the sections where daughters are mistreated, where women are property, where females are excluded from the priesthood or any other central role in our early history.

To be a rabbi and a woman is to stand in an acquired tradition that has been, at the same time, all mine and not at all mine. To be a rabbi and a woman is to teach that which has been received together with that which is yet to be received. It is my great hope that men will find themselves drawn into this woman's drama as revisionists too. I wrote this book with the prayer that I may do what Bible commentators have done in every age: to "reteach a thing its loveliness." That is the best of what we feminists are trying to do: not only to reteach ourselves, not only to reteach men, but to *reteach the Torah itself* its loveliness.

PART I

Women in the Torah

We All Stood Together

My brother and I were at Sinai
He kept a journal
of what he saw
of what he heard
of what it all meant to him

I wish I had such a record
of what happened to me there

It seems like every time I want to write
I can't
I'm always holding a baby
one of my own
or one for a friend
always holding a baby
so my hands are never free
to write things down

And then
as time passes
the particulars
the hard data
the who what when where why
slip away from me

and all I'm left with is
the feeling

But feelings are just sounds
the vowel barking of a mute

My brother is so sure of what he heard
after all he's got a record of it
consonant after consonant after consonant

If we remembered it together
we could recreate holy time
sparks flying

Merle Feld

Introduction

I wish it were this easy and this clear: "Women in the Torah are only wives, mothers and daughters. They are chattel." Or, equally easy and equally clear the other way: "Women in the Torah are exalted. Women in the Torah are portrayed completely positively." But neither statement is completely true.

The reality is that, in the Torah, women are complex, both subjects and objects. They are neither totally subjugated, denied their rights and suppressed; nor prominent, respected and powerful center-stage actors. The women of the Torah weave in and out of the frames of power and powerlessness. They act both as independent agents and as obedient dependents. They work within the patriarchal structure to change it for their own benefit, but they do not challenge the underlying structure of hierarchy and inequality for all women. They are fully human: they are curious, desirous, jealous, cooperative and co-opted. Sometimes they act like "stereotypical" women and sometimes they do not.

The underlying tension in the Torah is between women as "persons" and women as "property." In a polygamous society, women tend to be valued objects, like cattle or jewels—the more you have, the richer you appear to be. Women can be traded like commodities, given away or sold. Exodus 20: 14 lists women among the things a man "has." In Exodus 21: 7 a father may sell his daughter into slavery. According to Deuteronomy 22, a husband may publicly challenge his wife's virginity (and she has to stay married to him even if he is proved wrong by her father, who brings forth "tokens of her virginity" that is, a bloody bedsheet from the bridal chamber). A husband can cancel his wife's vows in Numbers 30, or publicly humiliate her if he even suspects her of adultery in Numbers 5.

Yet respect for a mother, no less than for a father, is one of the Ten Commandments. Five women together, the daughters of Tzelophehad, successfully change the inheritance laws to include daughters in Numbers 27. In Leviticus 14, no father can force his daughter to become a prostitute. Barren women, while depressed and desperate, are not cast off by their husbands or the tribe. The commandment to rest on the Sabbath applies equally to men and women. The Torah holds women to the same moral standards throughout its pages as men. And while the patriarchs of the five books of Moses are described as wealthy, all are monogamous except for Jacob, and he is polygamous not by his own design or will. Abraham listens to Sarah even though it means he has to force out Hagar. Rebecca secures the blessing for her favored son.

The contrast is striking. Women characters are portrayed as powerful, and yet they are subject to the authority of their husband or father. Women are also portrayed as powerless, yet daring, charismatic, strong and capable.

This ambivalence between women as persons and women as property, women as independent agents and women as dependent householders is best exemplified by the poem in Proverbs 31, usually translated as "A Woman of Valor." This poem is traditionally recited by a husband to his wife on the Sabbath eve. Feminists see it in both a positive and a negative light, and it is rich in symbolism of "ideal womanhood."

> A woman of valor—who can find? Her price is far above rubies. Her husband has confidence in her, and so he has no lack of gain. She does him good and not evil all the days of her life. She seeks wool and flax, and works willingly with her hands. She is like the merchant ships; she brings her food from afar. She rises while it is still night, and gives food to her household, and a portion to her maidens. She appraises a field

> and buys it; with the fruits of her own hands she plants a vineyard. She girds herself with strength and performs her tasks with vigor, she sees that her business thrives, and her lamp goes on far into the night. She takes hold of the distaff and her hands work the spindle. She stretches forth her palms to the poor and reaches forth her hands to the needy. She is not afraid of snow for her household; her whole household is clothed in scarlet. She makes coverlets for herself; all her clothing is fine linen and purple. Her husband is known in the gates, when he sits among the leaders of the land. She makes garments and sells them; she delivers girdles to the merchant. Strength and dignity clothe her, and she is cheerful about the future. She opens her mouth with wisdom, and words of kindness are on her tongue. She looks well to the ways of her household, and does not eat the bread of idleness. Her children declare her happy; her husband sings her praises: "Many daughters are valorous, but you excel them all." Charm is deceptive and beauty short-lived; but a woman who fears God shall be truly praised. Give her from the fruit of her hands; let her own deeds praise her in the gates. (Proverbs 31: 10–31)

This poem divides its view of woman into thirds: woman as wife and mother, woman as business manager and independent financial source, and woman as spiritual being. It begins by speaking of a "woman of worth." *Chayil*, a word usually reserved for men, connotes physical strength or might, a person "at the height of their powers and capabilities."[8] She is praised as a family member, a beacon of hope and light to her husband. Yet she is equally lauded for her business acumen, her ability to manage a field and sell its produce. When she appraises a field and then buys it, we wonder: how was she able to do this? With her own money? Did she ask her husband? "She girds herself with strength and performs her tasks with vigor, she sees that her business thrives, her lamp goes on far into the night." (It's as if she's staying up late at the computer, balancing the books and orders for the next day!) The poem extols her personhood, her inner strength and goodness. "Her children declare her happy," because she is happy. She is beautiful in a spiritual way. ("Beautiful" women are the result of cosmetics.) The poem seems to suggest that it is not her outer beauty that men should seek, as they so often do, but her inner spirit.

This is not a one-dimensional woman. This woman is as complex as we are today, and perhaps just as conflicted about her multiplicity of roles as we are. This portrait of woman is fully presented, and includes a valuing of her role as wife and mother, as business-woman, and as a woman of morality and goodness. The biblical storyteller here, as in other places, sees woman in the dual role of independent agent and attached subject. "Woman of Valor" acts as a paradigm, the themes of which appear throughout the Torah.

Power and Powerlessness

When we ask how much power biblical women had, we must first examine what women's power meant during biblical times. We should not assume our foremothers would have exercised power in the same way we do today. Did our female ancestors recognize the existing power structure as oppressive to them? Did they see themselves as preservers of that system or victims of it? Did the women who came before us see an escape from the system, or even want to see one? The appropriate question looms large: Does the system change women or do women change the system? As Paula Cooey has suggested, "Unless women transform the public, patriarchal institutions of which they become a part, and until we redefine the meaning of public and private in nonpatriarchal terms, the social order will remain patriarchal."[9] Do we want to be women in power who act, think, talk and even dress like men in power—or do we want to be "different" in our power roles?

We ask these questions about our matriarchs, albeit from our own modern vantage point. We feel disappointed when they do not transcend the limitations of their day. We feel excited when they do. We feminists want our foremothers to be feminist role models. If they transformed the system, we can too. If they challenged the existing order, we can too. If indeed they fit into our definition of feminist, the Torah recoups some beauty and meaning for us.

But if our foremothers transformed the system, it was only in small ways, circumscribed and cautious. Did the system change them? Women in biblical times were not allowed close enough to the center, as priests or heads of tribes, to answer that question. On one level, they exercised power in ways we would stereotype as "women's ways" but which we reject as true power. They manipulated, pleaded and deceived. Yet on another level, they indeed did exercise true power. They decided, organized and resisted, which must have been difficult, given the cultural expectations of proper female behavior in their day.

Our generation of women in newly found positions of power need new role models, new visions of what power is and what it means. We often experience power, yet abhor the patriarchal dominion and control that power connotes. We feel the same ambivalence toward power I imagine our female predecessors did. As Cooey writes,

> Power that transforms people and bonds them with one another in communities calls in question prevailing conceptions of power as an exercise in control, particularly political, social, and economic control . . . Dynamic tension between an experience of transformation as empowering, on the one hand, and feelings of ambivalence towards power on the other hand, provides the possibility for critical affirmation and continued creativity . . . 10

On the one hand, our foremothers existed and were controlled within the structures of their day, and this control affected their ability to ultimately transform those structures. On the other hand, our foremothers achieved success in their attempt to transform people and bond them to one another.

Interestingly, many male biblical characters work alone or, when in relationship, are in conflict with one another. Abraham barely speaks to his son Isaac as they walk up the mountain in the episode of the near-sacrifice. Cain and Abel, Jacob and Esau are adversaries. Isaac and Ishmael, the two sons of Abraham, were once close, but end up separated. In contrast, we observe the cooperative efforts of sisters Leah and Rachel when it is time to leave Laban's house, the daughters of Tzelophehad who organize in the desert and claim an inheritance of their father's land, and the women of the Exodus story who unite against Pharaoh. These are models of "power that transforms people and bonds them with one another in communities."

Sometimes it feels as if the question of biblical women and their power is a political one. It depends not on *what* you are asking, but *why*. Are we trying to prove that women were equal to men in biblical society, that women had what they needed, participated fully? Or are we trying to prove that women were subservient and downtrodden? I reject the theory that as "the power behind the throne" (as manipulators of men) women hold true power. But I do not reject that this methodology of gaining control may have been the only one open and available to our foremothers in the Torah. I see our foremothers as powerful *in their own context, though not in mine.*

How do we define an individual's real power? Is it use of one's ability to manipulate, convince or coerce? Is it charisma? Is it knowledge? Is it leadership skills? If our definition includes all these characteristics, then the matriarchs and other women of the Torah wove themselves in and out of power. Sharon Ringe charges that

> women are thus absent from the Bible as persons working out their own religious journeys . . . Rather, women appear—to use a metaphor from grammar—as direct and indirect 'objects' and not as 'subjects' of the verbs of religious experience and practice . . . women are often 'flat' characters, perfectly good or villainously evil, or objects at someone's disposal.[11]

If we look carefully at the following Torah stories, and allow the characters to speak in their own voices—the only voices they had, in the language of their times—they will not appear flat at all. Instead, these women act with great courage and wisdom; they are neither perfectly good nor villainously evil. Tzipporah, the midwives, Miriam, Yocheved and the daughter of Pharaoh, Leah and Rachel, the five daughters of Tzelophehad may seem like "supporting actors," but they are not merely walk-ons. The lens through which we have seen them has been a male one, a rabbinic tradition that has valued and extensively written about their femininity. In that context, their strength has been devalued, or more likely never even investigated.

Because this book is a general overview of the issues around feminism and the Torah, and because it would take an entire book on its own to fully explore each and every female personality who is either named or unnamed in the Torah, I have chosen only a few women upon whom we will focus. These are the women I see as prototypes, as examples of female activists in the biblical period manifesting some semblance of true power. The female characters I have chosen are rich and alive, complicated and complex. Of course, we want Eve to name herself. How wonderful if Rachel and Leah had spoken out against polygamy. Of course we wish the women of the Exodus story had risen up against the oppression of all women, as well as all Jews. But the Torah is not a perfect drama with Hollywood-style endings and political correctness. Its greatness is that it contains the struggles that we still experience today, the evil that we still see today, the frustrations that we still feel today. Its women are single, married, mothers and wives, friends. They argue, they cry, they flee, they fight. Anything else would truly be flat.

Woman as person or woman as property? Both. Woman as powerful or woman as powerless? Both. Unsatisfying as that answer may be for those who want black or white, we shall see this gray area over and over again. It is as if the Torah cannot make up its mind; as if God has not yet decided and declared. And is not our society today still ambivalent, and in the same way?

Male and Female Were They Created: Eve, Lilith and the Snake

> And God said: Let us make a "being" (in Hebrew—adam) in our image, like us. They shall rule the fish of the sea and the fowl of the air,

> the cattle, the whole earth and all that creeps on the earth. So God created "the being" in God's image, in the image of God was it made; male and female were they made. God blessed them and said, Be fruitful and multiply . . . (Genesis 1: 26–27)

> And the Lord God said, "It is not good for the being to be alone; I will make a helper opposite [or: beside] him" . . . so the Lord God cast a deep slumber upon the being and he slept; and God took one of his ribs [or: sides] and closed up the flesh at that spot. And the Lord God built a woman from that taken rib [or: side] and brought her to the being. And the being said: "This time this one is bone of my bones and flesh of my flesh; this one shall be called woman, for from man was this one taken." (Genesis 2: 18–23)

Creation

I never learnt that first creation story in Sunday school. I do not ever recall it being explained, interpreted or discussed from the pulpit. I do remember it being taken for granted that the tale of Adam and Eve and the rib was *the* creation story. Ask any child today about the beginnings of humanity and you will probably get the rib story. Art, literature and poetry speak of Eve from the rib. The rib, the rib, always the rib. (The Hebrew word translated as rib, *tzela*, can also mean side. Woman created from man's side changes the dynamic a bit.) We act as if the rib story is the Torah's only way—and thus the only correct way—of looking at woman as spiritual being, created from and part of man.

The critical message of the first chapter of the first book of the Torah is not the rib. It is just the opposite. Both woman and man are born as equals from a genderless but fertile God. Imagine if I had learnt this version of creation as a young girl in Sunday school! Since Judaism was so important to my family, and since we were grounded in our ethics being Jewish ethics, this would have been my earliest lesson in the morality of equality. I would have seen my own equality with little boys as Divinely ordained and Jewishly correct. That would have been a powerful lesson.

The Torah begins with a description of a world about to become. This as yet unformed universe is chaotic, percolating, volcanic and void. The creation is described, but the creator is not. The Divine Being who steps into the narrative is taken for granted. The reader seems to know already who it is or what it is. Without introduction, the text simply calls the creator "Elohim," the Hebrew generic word for God. The reader is not informed who this God is, or how God came to be. This God becomes known not through descriptions of what this God *is*, but through descriptions of what this God *does*.

What God does—the forming of this shapeless world into Earth—happens through speech. In contrast to the mythologies of other Near Eastern gods and goddesses, this Creator appears fairly sexless; it does not "birth" the world from an act of coupling, but begets the world in a manner divorced from sexuality, through an act powered by words. God is productive, without being sexually reproductive. While male-gendered terms—adjectives and pronouns—are the norm in the biblical narrative, the Creator is not described as being *a male*. God has no genitals, no sex organs, no male or female consort. Sexuality is reserved for humanity, and God is differentiated from us by this ability to produce without intercourse. As J.A. Phillips writes, "Yahweh's realm is not nature but history . . . The world and all that is in it is the work of his fingers, but in no sense his offspring."[12]

After establishing the animal and natural world, God turns to the task of making humanity, also accomplished through speech.

The whole picture in this first chapter of Genesis is of lush fertility, using images like the gathering of waters; the expanse of heaven; and the swarming, flying and swimming of many kinds of creatures. The human being is produced in a way similar to the other beings which populate this new world.

This first being, called in Hebrew *adam*, is both male and female. In fact, there is a grammatical fluidity between the singular "it" and plural "they" when the text refers to the creature *adam*, as if it could be either one being or two, or one combined being. The animals are then blessed with fecundity, and so too the first human. As the earth brings forth vegetation, so too the human being will produce seed. The being is blessed, and commanded to be fruitful and multiply. However, it is not clear *with whom* the being is to be fruitful and multiply. With the animals? Since the being is both male and female, does the text assume it will multiply with itself? Perhaps, like God, the being will reproduce without sexuality, through speech, mirroring the Divine paradigm of creation.

Or perhaps the Divine paradigm is different from what we have thought. Since Genesis 1 states clearly that the human being is in God's image and the human being is male *and* female, it follows that God's image—and God—must be both male and female. The Hebrew term "Elohim" used in Genesis 1 is a plural form, although traditionally considered grammatically to be singular, like the English word "group." The verb that follows it, except in two rare cases, is always in the singular. One could argue homiletically, however, that the choice of what seems on a simple level to be a plural form for the very first reference to God in the text is no accident. It has a purpose. All former gods and goddesses are absorbed into this one God. Both male and female qualities are contained in this God. As the human being encompasses both masculine and feminine, so too does the Divine Being. If God reproduced the world through the fusing of the male and female aspects of Divinity, then, like God, the human being can reproduce through the fusing of its own two sides, male and female.

Knowing that "Elohim" for God is viewed as singular, the classical Jewish commentators were puzzled and disturbed by the plural form of God's utterance "let *us* make humanity in *our* image." In their refusal to let the Jewish Torah be seen as a proof of Christianity's trinity, and in their rejection of the possibility that the Torah might have positive references to the polytheistic beliefs of the culture surrounding the Hebrews, they explained away all possibilities of the plurality of God. They suggested that the plural here was "the royal we," or God speaking with the angels. I suggest we hear God's internal dialogue, the female and male aspects of Divinity in conversation with each other, checking to be sure both sides are represented in the creation of humanity.

In this first chapter of Genesis, hierarchy is also created to bring order into the chaos: the greater light to dominate the day, the lesser light to dominate the night; the being to rule, fill and master the earth. But there is as yet no male/female hierarchy. Man neither rules nor dominates woman. Neither the male nor the female has a "proper name" yet, and the man does not name the woman, as he will in a later chapter. In this first depiction of the new world lies the clear *idea* of inherent equality. This idyllic Eden is one of equality, of fertile ground and fertile nature, of symmetry and harmony.

The second chronicle of creation, in Genesis chapter 2, refashions everything. In this variation on the theme, in the place of one bigendered being, there is woman created from man. As if unaware of previous traditions or tales, the narrative presents a wholly new explanation of humanity's beginnings. In the first tale we have the birth of humanity from Divinity, a birth that is miraculous but free of sex and gender. Neither man nor woman is the progenitor. But in the rib tale, man gives birth, as it were, from his own body. In this account woman is created second. She is born from the man, and not he from her.

Feminist interpreters continue to debate the meaning of this second account. Phyllis Trible argues that since man is sleeping when woman is created "he is neither participant nor spectator nor consultant at her birth."[13] But certainly this story tells us something new about the nature of humanity. Woman is now "helper," and "taken" from man. Here we see the first source of woman's otherness. If woman is taken from an already created man, then woman as a "class" is a part of, dependent upon, and perceived as fundamentally connected to man. The theological justification for women's sociological subordination now becomes textual. Thus, in this version of humanity's creation, the "proper" hierarchy of male and female is also created. This hierarchy later finds expression in everything from the laws of women's marital responsibilities to the metaphor of the God/Israel relationship, where God takes the role of husband and Israel takes the role of wife.

And why the rib? A midrash, a rabbinic parable or tale, suggests that "the rib is a hidden part of the body, and therefore it was chosen to teach women modesty."[14] Not only does the conception of woman from man create a new impression in the religious theory of humanity's origins, but the choice of the rib profoundly influences later rabbinic notions of women's role.

In this second story, we have the gendering of humanity, with the "invention" of a woman. Here the words for man and for woman, as gendered and separate individuals, are used for the first time in the Hebrew Torah: *ish* and *ishah*. Now "the being" is no longer neutral or androgynous. Only with the origin of woman as distinct and different is the being male, and we hear of that first creature as *a man*. By removing the female, the male is possible. Maleness now exists in relation to femaleness.

In the latter account, "the being" is sexually male, and this gendered creature, differentiated from woman for the first time, becomes her husband—in Hebrew *ba'al*, or master. It is possible for the male to be master only when he is no longer integrally part of the female. The institution of marriage introduced after this second account restores the male/female balance once so organic, when man and woman were literally one flesh. Thus, man and woman must rejoin through marriage to be joined as they were in the beginning of creation. So the Torah asserts "a man leaves his father and his mother and clings to his wife and they shall become as one flesh." As woman was taken from man in the beginning, she will be taken by him in marriage. (The expression in the Torah for marriage is "when a man *takes* a woman in marriage.")

Adam, remembering and yearning for the return of his lost duality, immediately recognizes the woman as a "fitting helpmate"—in Hebrew, *ezer kinegdo*. He does not want a "buddy." He wants a partner, his opposite or "other side." He wants back his feminine equivalent, his feminine side.

He and his wife have sex and produce a child. Fertility happens not with words, as it once did. Maleness and femaleness in humanity is, from here on, a factor that will shape personalities in the Torah. Marriage, fertility and infertility, fruitfulness and barrenness will become the central themes of the lives of most of the rest of the female characters in the Torah. Eden is forever changed.

In the first creation tale, the command to reproduce is given to "the being," male and female together. In the second tale of Adam and Eve, it is gendered men and women who sexually reproduce. It is amazing, then, to see how the later Rabbis of the

Talmud proclaimed that the commandment to "be fruitful and multiply" was incumbent only upon men! They claimed women would, of course, normally choose to marry and bear children. But men, they teach, need this first commandment to be almost forced upon them. It domesticates them, as it were, to the notion of the responsibility to reproduce. Men would not choose to father the way women would choose to mother, so they must be commanded to do so.[15]

The traditional commentators were perplexed by the contradiction apparent when the two stories, one of innate equality and one of woman as "helper," are placed together. They wanted to prove that the two stories are not individual accounts, reflecting a change in society's outlook or a male refiguring. Rashi suggests that, in the first narrative, the being was made with two faces or two sides. Because it was the sixth day, God rushed to finish before the Sabbath, and could only create man and woman together! Thus the Torah doesn't fill in the details of their respective gender identities until a later chapter, when the two sides are split.

According to Rashi, God went back to "finish the job." A midrash suggests that God originally created the one being as male and female, but while s/he slept, God detached the female part of his back and replaced the missing part with flesh. Philo, the Jewish philosopher of the first century C.E., thought that the "first Adam" never existed at all, but was a formed *idea* rather than a formed *man*. The original Adam was "pure mind," but when joined to Eve, in the second chapter, became flesh and therefore earthly. On the basis of Greek thinking, with which Philo was very familiar, we see the identification of woman with body, man with intellect.

Some modern biblical exegetes have attempted to integrate the two stories as both representative of egalitarianism, suggesting that since the Hebrew term *ezer*, a "helper," can also mean "power," *ezer kinegdo* is not "a fitting helper" but "a power equal to him."Thus both stories can be seen as containing the idea of gender equality.[16]

But what happened to that first, equal woman of Genesis 1? Where is she when Eve comes along in Genesis 2? Perhaps the cleverest attempt at answering that question is the midrash of Lilith. Inventing her from the Hebrew word for night, *laila*, the rabbis wrote about Lilith as the original female creation. The rabbis already knew the word *Lilith* from the one place it appears in the Hebrew Bible, Isaiah 34: 14, where she is at rest with satyrs and hyenas in the wilderness. Perhaps they also knew an earlier mythological prototype, the she-devil, the demon who destroys children. They picture her as utterly fearsome and yet utterly alone.

Knowing the first woman was made at the same time as the first man, and of the same substance, the rabbis assume she would insist on equality. The midrash does not mince words: she demands a chance to have sex with her on top! Adam refuses and pleads with God to send him a new, better wife. Lilith is banished from the garden.

With Lilith gone, God realizes that "it is not good for the being to be alone," and God creates a new being, this time not from the same substance as Adam, but from Adam himself. When she is brought to him for inspection, no wonder the being exclaims, "This time [as opposed to the first time] this one [as opposed to Lilith] is [quite literally] bone of my bones and flesh of my flesh."The fictional Lilith releases the rabbis from any notion of the primacy of the first text. Appearing in later rabbinic literature as the feared independent woman who hates men, despises and destroys male babies and brings disaster to marriages, she proves in the rabbinic world-view that the first try at equality was a mistake.[17]

The creation of Eve, now seen as the preferable role model in place of Lilith, corrects that mistake for all women. The first woman was simply the wrong one to become the mother of all life! "This one shall be called woman"—this one certainly, for the first one was called *adam* together with him. A name for this new creature must be found. She is not named for the substance—earth—as before. She is not even named for the substance from which she was made: "from the *tzela*." She is named for her relationship to man—"for from man was she taken."

> And the being called his woman's [or: wife's] name Eve [in Hebrew—*Hava*, meaning life or living], because she was the mother of all that is living. (Genesis 3: 20)

Taken from man, she is named by man. Naming symbolizes control. As Adam achieves dominion over the animals he has named, so too he asserts it over the woman. The lesson of the first story of original equality is now obscured. The being gives *his* woman—for in this context she is no longer just *the* woman—a proper name. As God named light, the first separated entity from dark, Adam names woman, the separate being from man. As light is unlike dark, so she is unlike him. She will be linked to the rest of humanity through her female fruitfulness, even though when she receives this name *she has not yet borne children!* Her name is descriptive of the female place, the female role, the female "nature."

> This is the record of *adam's* lineage when God created *adam* in the Divine likeness; male and female were they created. God blessed them and called their name Adam in the day God made them. (Genesis 5: 1–2)

The Eden narrative ends with a summary of events and a genealogical table. This concluding verse in Genesis 5 is a translator's nightmare! *Adam* is both a generic term, meaning "a being," and a proper name, "Adam." The name of the man we have come to identify as "Adam" is also *adam* in Hebrew, a word play on *adama*, meaning earth. At the summation of the Eden stories, in the fifth chapter of Genesis, *adam* seems to be used in both senses: to identify the original unnamed male/female being and to also identify the male being of the rib story. The reader is reminded here that *adam* was created both male and female, and then God names them *both* with the proper name of Adam. Here, in the final "credits" to the Eden episodes, the Torah deliberately harks back to and reiterates the original saga of equality. In the reader's, or listener's mind, Adam the man is melded into *adam*, the dual being. It is almost as if the rib tale were itself a midrash, an elaboration, an imaginative excursus on the first story of equal creation.

Modern scholars conjecture that Genesis 1 and 2 were two totally disparate creation stories woven together by a later editor. Perhaps the first narrative in 1, and this "reminder" in Genesis 5, together form an older unit from a time of remembered parity, a time before patriarchy. This unit is a kind of dream put in by those who wished that kind of society to be made real. Maybe the Torah intended both units, seemingly contradictory, to be placed together to teach us about the tension between biological equality and societal, cultural expectations and limitations based on gender. The first creation narrative certainly suggests both the dual nature of all human beings and the integrated oneness of all human beings.

If we analyze the two variants through the generalized lens with which men and women look at the world, the first story is women's: one of existential relationship and connection, of the interweaving of self and other. The rib story is men's: one of separation and detachment overcome through sexual union. Perhaps the rib story was included as a theological statement of the way things are and ought to be. Or maybe it just made a better story, closer to home and yet more dramatic.

The rib story brings us an explanation of gender, of why men and women are different and play different roles in society. It justifies the hierarchy our ancestors were beginning to experience. And the snake story, which follows, seals that explanation of gender roles with a description of a new enmity between man and woman.

The Snake

> And the Lord God commanded the being, "Of every tree of the garden you are free to eat, but of the tree of knowledge of good and evil, do not eat for the day you eat of it you will die." (Genesis 2: 16)

Did Eve hear this command? Two verses *later*, in 2: 18, God causes the man to sleep and woman to be formed of his rib. If we accept the duality of the first creation account, that the being is still both male and female, then the female "side" heard the precept not to eat of the forbidden tree. Let us suppose then that the woman was fully aware of the commandment when she made the decision to disobey. That would certainly change the traditional reading of Eve and the serpent and the taking of the fruit. Newly separated from Adam, she needs to assert her own selfhood. Joined together, they made joint decisions. Now that she is on her own, she leads, she decides, she experiments. When she tastes the fruit, she tastes independence.

Or, if we accept the veracity of the Lilith midrash, that the first female being has already been banished from the garden, then this is the second woman, the more docile Eve, who is easily beguiled by the snake. Lilith returns to whisper in Eve's ear: "The more you know, the more you are. Knowledge is power, ignorance is eternal subservience. Eat the fruit!" Traditional mythology has always linked the serpent with woman—Medusa with the serpent hair. Maybe the snake is Lilith.

Or the snake is Eve's female consciousness. The snake symbolizes woman, the female yearning to be bound not by rules, by *thou shalts* and *thou shalt nots*, but by trust and by relationship. The tree, phallic in appearance, represents phallic authority, the male system of rules and regulations. The fruit, round and female, represents a circle, a cycle, life based on connections. That female fruit gets disconnected from the male tree as Eve becomes disconnected from her male/female self.

The woman chooses the fruit. And there is, to be sure, a punishment for that choice. The punishments handed to the man and woman parallel each other poetically. The man must physically labor to get the earth to produce, and the woman, a symbol of earth, must physically labor to get herself to produce.

In contrast to its female symbolism, in other ancient cultures the snake has also symbolized the phallus. A hostility originates between women and the snake to last forever, a symbol of the perpetual and ongoing male/female struggle. It is as if she knows, and God knows too, that with this second ordering of the hierarchy of genders there can no longer be the peace and harmony of the first androgyny. The original Eden is now long gone.

Though the punishment includes the pronouncement that woman's desire will be for her husband and he will "rule" over her, in fact the Hebrew word for rule, *yimshol*, can be understood in an entirely different way. The root *ma-sha-l* also means an example, a model. "Your desire shall be for your husband, and he shall *model himself after you*." He will cherish your commitment to monogamy, your ability to find sexual satisfaction with just one partner. In you, he will have a role model of fidelity and sexual stability.

With a woman, a man learns by example what proper desire is. Woman not only begins the partnership of creation, which until now was God's alone, she also offers a new vision of humanness that harkens back to God's original plan. In this homiletic reading of her punishment lies the seed of the redemption of male–female relationships. Let men model themselves after women sexually. Perhaps then we can get back to the first harmony we had when we were joined as one.

Many scholarly studies of the creation story see, in this tree story, a story of punishment and banishment, an Eve "defeated" by Adam. This once-free spirit, independent Eve, is now "mastered" by her husband. J.A. Phillips writes, "It is as though the writers believed that civilization could not begin or be sustained until the Feminine, as a dominant religious power, had been mastered and domesticated."[18] Eve can be seen as the symbol of the social domestication of woman. Now woman is subordinate, and we can see why. Femaleness associated with man's dominion over and mastery of woman and gender as a defining, limiting border is now firmly established.

But this border can end where it began: Men and women are intended by the Torah to be as they first were, beings created together and equally in the Divine image. Although we live in a gendered world, that world was created later, almost as a second thought, as a midrash on the first world. Gender is a social construct created by the separation between men and women. It does not exist in the first reading of Genesis, where the dual gender of the being does not define, restrict or enlarge; there are no rights, responsibilities or roles associated with the being's male or femaleness.

The first narrative of inherent equality in the Divine image should be the focus of a feminist rereading of those days in Eden. It should be taught and preached as the "real" creation story. Imagine the difference it would make to girls and women hearing that they are not secondary in God's plan. Imagine the ennoblement of women as they learn from earliest childhood that the original plan of God's universe is the ultimate equality of men and women. Men would have to rethink what has been assumed to be God's order. Those of us who live and work in the religious realm should begin a program for change that would include God's very first wish, that man and woman, of the same substance, finally be at one, as it was "In the Beginning."

Leah and Rachel: A Study in Relationships

The Torah is full of stories of sibling rivalry. Brothers fight with brothers. Brothers vie for inheritance. Brothers cheat each other, usurp each other, flee from each other. The sibling stories in the Torah concentrate on brothers, or a combination of brothers and father, brothers and mother, or brothers with a sister. Biblical society is as much a fraternity as a patriarchy. The stories of Leah and Rachel are noteworthy because they present a unique picture of a relationship between sisters.

There are other sisters in the Torah, but they are sisters to men. Rebecca, our second matriarch, has a brother named Laban. When Isaac wants to marry Rebecca, Laban takes over the marriage plans, acting more like a father than a brother. Laban assumes the role of head of the family, relating to Rebecca rather paternally. (Some commentators suggest that her father, Bethuel, had already died.) The relationship of this sister and brother is not well developed.

Dinah is a sister to the twelve sons of Jacob, and her relationship with them after her rape by Shechem in Genesis 34 is that of a wronged victim and her protectors. We learn nothing of her relationship to them before that incident, and nothing thereafter. The brothers react to the rape of their sister violently and punitively, because they feel *themselves* shamed by the act perpetrated upon her. They too act in a patronizing manner. The text says nothing about Dinah's feelings toward them, and does not record her reaction to their act of retaliation.

In Miriam's story, we see some development of a sibling rivalry between Moses and his sister, exacerbated by Aaron's role as high priest. Moses is the leader of the Israelites, Aaron the appointed chief of the sacrificial cult. Miriam's leadership role is not clearly defined, though the text recognizes her as a prophetess. In Numbers 12, after she complains about Moses' monopoly of power and is punished with leprosy for this confrontation, Moses prays for her recovery only after Aaron begs him to. Whether Moses and Miriam are a team, or rivals, is not obvious from the text.

There are only two stories of a group of sisters, and no rivalry is recorded in either case. They seem to live together and work together. The first group is the daughters of Jethro, who are mentioned briefly when the eldest is chosen as a wife for Moses. That is all we hear of them. Though the famous movie *The Ten*

Commandments contains a scene of the girls competing for Moses, nothing of the sort appears in the actual Torah text.

In Numbers 26, the second group of sisters is the daughters of Tzelophehad, who work together to change the laws of inheritance. We will examine shortly how they approach Moses as a team. However, we learn nothing of the relationship between them as sisters. The story treats them as a unit rather than as individuals.

Thus, Leah and Rachel are the sole example of two sisters in relationship. Their stories in Genesis 29, 30 and 31 paint a realistic picture of the life of sisters: jealousy, sacrifice, love, sadness and accommodation. Their powerlessness lies in their relationship with Laban, their father, who manipulates them and Jacob. The three together demonstrate strong will against him when they leave his household. Their relationship to Jacob is fraught with tension, understandable for two sisters married to the same man. Yet they work together when it becomes clear that fertility is the way for both of them to gain what they want. They seem trapped in patriarchal assumptions of their value, yet they take decisive action to ensure their future.

> While he was still speaking with them, Rachel came with her father's flock, for she was a shepherdess. And when Jacob saw Rachel, the daughter of his uncle Laban, and the flock of his uncle Laban, Jacob went up and rolled the stone off the mouth of the well, and watered the flock of his uncle Laban. Then Jacob kissed Rachel, and broke into tears. (Genesis 29: 9–11)

Jacob meets Rachel at the well, as his father, Isaac, had met Rebecca at a well, and as Moses will meet Tzipporah at a well. Our expectations of romance are raised as we watch and see what will happen between these two. It is love at first sight, exactly as it was with Jacob's mother and father before him. To win Rachel, Jacob must first unroll the stone that closes up the water. That stone represents Rachel's barrenness, the heavy burden that must be overturned in order for her to produce.

We learn quickly that Rachel is a shepherdess, which means that she will be outdoors, among shepherds and other men. Although she is the younger of Laban's two daughters, she comes alone to the well, a place known to attract many men, and sometimes rough ones. She must be well respected and well known among the shepherds who are already at the well, for they herald her arrival to Jacob. Jacob's kiss does not faze her, but the news that he is kin to her (and therefore a good prospect for marriage) causes her to run in excitement to her father.

> When he had stayed with him a month's time, Laban said to Jacob, "Just because you are my kin, should you serve me for nothing? Tell me, what shall your wages be?" Now Laban had two daughters; the name of the older one was Leah and the name of the younger one was Rachel. Leah had soft eyes; Rachel was extremely beautiful. Jacob loved Rachel, so he answered, "I will serve you seven years for your younger daughter, Rachel." Laban said, "Better I should give her to you than to an outsider. Stay with me." So Jacob served seven years for Rachel and they seemed to him but a few days because of his love for her. Then Jacob said to Laban, "Give me my wife, for my time is over and I may go in to her." Then Laban gathered all the people of the place and made a feast. When evening came, he took his daughter Leah and brought her to him, and he cohabited with her. (Laban had given his maidservant Zilpah to his daughter Leah as a maid.) When morning came, there was Leah! He said to Laban, "What is this that you have

> done to me? I was in your service for Rachel! Why did you deceive me?" Laban said, "It is not the practice in our place to give the younger before the older. Wait until the bridal week of this one is over and we will give you the other one too, provided you serve me another seven years. Jacob did so: the bridal week of that one was fulfilled and then he gave him his daughter Rachel as a wife. (Genesis 29: 14–27)

The sisters are introduced together here, although we have already met Rachel. We did not know when we met her earlier at the well that she had an older sister. This juxtaposition of them in the introduction foreshadows their interconnectedness. Sharon Pace Jeansonne notes, "It will not be the only time they are compared, and the irony soon will unfold. Although Rachel is beautiful, it is Leah who is fertile. Rachel's value to Jacob as a beautiful wife is apparent, whereas Leah's ability to bear children is hidden."[19] Unknown to him when he first meets Rachel at the well, hidden from him as she walks into the marriage tent, Leah and her eyes become symbols of what Jacob cannot, or will not see. She is his own deceit come back to repay him, restoring the natural order of the older before the younger. Through Laban, Jacob is the recipient of the classic "bait and switch," the leitmotif of many of the sibling stories before and after him.

This theme of trickery plays itself out strongly in the narrative. Jacob, who tricked his brother Esau, gets tricked by Laban. Jacob, the younger who supplanted the older, tries again in his new family, attempting to marry the younger before the older. In classic Jewish thought, this is *middah k'neged middah*, Jacob's own acts of subversion with Esau coming back now to haunt him in another guise. He, who once tricked others, gets tricked himself. He must first marry Leah, the older daughter, and he resents it.

Laban reminds him that he has no right to complain. He now receives retribution for having overtaken his older brother.

Before the marriages, we hear nothing of Leah and Rachel's relationship to each other. We wonder how Laban was able to "take" Leah and "give" her to Jacob. We wonder if she consented or was forced. Did she see this marriage as a way out of loneliness? Or a way out of her father's repressive house? Why did she not go to the well with her sister to meet the eligible young bachelors?

The commentators suggest she was unmarriageable because of her eyes, which are said to be *racot*. Usually translated as "weak" or "ugly" it can also mean "tender." The text is not explicit as to whether the word has negative connotations of ugly or the positive connotation of tender, but surely the narrator is trying to juxtapose Rachel's appearance with Leah's.

Leah should have Jacob—just as Esau should have had that birthright and Ishmael should have had his inheritance. She is the "rightful" first marriage. We suspect she must resent Rachel for being Jacob's chosen one. How did Rachel feel seeing her sister enter the marriage tent that evening? Was Rachel even aware of the switch, or did Laban do it quickly and quietly? On all this the text is silent, but a midrash fills in the story. In the Talmudic rendition of the story, it was Rachel, not her father, who commandeered the switch.

> Jacob said to Rachel, "Will you marry me?" She replied to him, "Yes, but father is a trickster, and you will not be able to hold your own against him." "Wherein does his sharp dealing lie?" asked Jacob. She said, "I have a sister who is older than I, and he will not allow me to be married before her." "I am his brother in sharp dealings." said Jacob . . . So he entrusted Rachel with special signs. While Leah was being led

> into the bridal chamber, Rachel thought, "My sister will now be disgraced," and so she entrusted her with these same signs. And this accounts for the Scriptural text, "When morning came, there was Leah!" This is the explanation: On account of the signs which Jacob had entrusted to Rachel who had entrusted them to Leah, he knew not who she was until that moment.[20]

The midrash does not tell us what those special signs were, but whatever secret code or marking or item Jacob entrusted to Rachel is shared with Leah. In this midrash it is Rachel who deceives both her father *and* Jacob, for the sake of her sister Leah. In this midrash Rachel refuses to let Leah be humiliated, and willingly gives up her place as the "first wife." She admits that her sister should be married first, and knows her father will do anything to ensure it. So instead, she herself ensures it.

The rabbis were so enamored of this midrash and their portrayal of Rachel as a loyal sister that they made her a role model of equanimity. In another midrash they picture Rachel, much later after her death, arguing with God from heaven in the wake of the golden calf episode. As she championed her sister's cause, she is pictured as championing the cause of Israel, especially in times of trouble.

> You know when my father planned to switch Leah for me I was not jealous nor did I bring her out in shame. I'm only flesh and blood, dust and ashes. So why are You, an Eternal and Merciful Ruler, jealous of such idolatry that has no significance? . . . And God answered, "Because of you, Rachel, I will restore Israel to its place."[21]

It took until the morning for Jacob to see. The word for the wedding feast in Hebrew is *mishteh*, which comes from the root "to drink," so it could be that Jacob was just too drunk at the feast to recognize Leah. Or perhaps Jacob knows it is Leah, but he wants very badly to think it is Rachel. In the dark he pretends. In the morning he has to face the truth.

It makes sense, in a way, that Jacob should marry Rachel. The Hebrew word *rachel* means ewe, and evokes a pastoral scene fitting for Jacob the shepherd. Jacob, the more feminine of the two brothers (Esau is the hunter and Jacob the "dweller in tents"), marries the little lamb.

But Leah also needs to marry Jacob, to complete the story. The midrash relates how Leah was meant to marry Esau, as both of them were the first born. She, however, refused to marry such a boor, crying copious tears anticipating her fate, which explains her weak eyes. By marrying Jacob, she is not only spared from that lot, but she also becomes a matriarch of the Jewish people through the sons she bears Jacob, sons who later become the tribes of Israel.

> The Lord saw that Leah was unloved and so opened her womb; but Rachel was barren . . . When Rachel saw that she had borne no children to Jacob, she became envious of her sister, and Rachel said to Jacob, "Give me children or I will die." (Genesis 29:31 and 30:1)

The younger supplants the older only in Jacob's love. Leah, though unloved by Jacob, will be "loved" by society for her gift of children. God rewards Leah with fertility to make up for her troubles with her husband, and the women are now equalized. One gets a man's love; the other gets a child's love. One gets status through a husband; the other gets status through children.

After Leah bears four sons, Rachel becomes desperate. Although the text reminds us that she is the loved one, she is not satisfied, so she gives Jacob her handmaid as a surrogate. The women name their children reflecting the contest between them. Reuben means "God has seen to a son for me," Naftali means "A fateful contest I have waged with my sister and won," Gad means "What luck!" and so on. Each name seems to say, "Oh good! Another one for me!" But somehow the reader still wonders if this is the real relationship between the women. Soon they will talk.

> Once, at the time of the wheat harvest, Reuben came upon some mandrakes in the field and brought them to his mother, Leah. Rachel said to Leah, "Please give me some of your son's mandrakes." But she answered her, "Was it not enough for you to take away my husband, that you would also take my son's mandrakes?" Rachel replied, "I promise, he shall lie with you tonight, in return for your son's mandrakes." (Genesis 30: 14–15)

This is the first dialogue between the sisters. Rachel is desperate for children, Leah for love. Since each is feeling hopeless, they can strike a bargain. Apparently Reuben is aware of the fertility competition between his mother and Rachel, for he brings mandrakes, an ancient aphrodisiac, directly to Leah. Leah knows these mandrakes could help Rachel's infertility, as mandrakes were considered in the ancient world to have reproductive healing power. Rachel speaks politely and somewhat hesitantly, using the word "please," and emphasizing the fact that the mandrakes belong to Leah's son. She knew that Reuben had those mandrakes, which suggests that the women spent some time together out in the field.

They finally speak. Leah shows her exasperation and frustration. Rachel tries to smooth things out. Rachel's offer to pay for mandrakes with sex with Jacob shows her power in determining with whom Jacob will sleep and suggests that through the years

Rachel is not only more loved by Jacob, but more sought out by him sexually. Sharon Pace Jeansonne notes, "It is ironic that the women whose lives were circumscribed by their scheming father and insensitive husband presently control Jacob's sexual activity."[22]

This tense exchange should not be overlooked for its subplot. Ilana Pardes suggests, "Jacob here descends to the humiliating position of being a token of exchange between two women . . . The eponymous father of Israel becomes the faithful mirror of his wives: the two sisters were exactly in this position when they were circulated between Laban and Jacob in Genesis 29."[23] They both display a muted anger at Jacob during this encounter over the mandrakes. Jacob is not giving love to Leah, nor is he giving children to Rachel. The women seem to be joining forces, working as a team, each for her own ends.

After Rachel gives birth, we hear the sisters speak in one united voice. Early rivalry between Leah and Rachel mirrors the rivalry between Jacob and Esau; it was essentially a struggle for power between immature actors. Now that Jacob is ready to meet Esau as a mature man, and now that his wives are mothers, they are ready to communicate with each other also as mature women. In Genesis 31, Jacob approaches them both about leaving Laban's house and they agree together to depart. They speak of Laban's amassed wealth as their own and their children's. They counsel Jacob to go and do what God has commanded. They leave their father, distraught over the injustices he has done to them.

Leah and Rachel leave together, powerful against their father. In some way, marrying Jacob has allowed them to leave the house of their father who has mocked and tricked them all. Rachel has the last laugh when she steals her father's household idols. The reader laughs too when she mocks him by sitting on them in the camel bag, claiming she has her period so she cannot get up to greet him.

In contrast, however, to other brotherly sibling rivalry stories where there is a clear victor—Cain over Abel, Isaac over Ishmael, Jacob over Esau, Joseph over his brothers—nobody really wins in this story. At first we pity poor Leah, but she quickly gains through her childbearing. So we end up pitying poor Rachel, loved but barren. There is a flux of the listener's sympathy. We never get to side totally with one or the other. All we can say is that Jacob seems to win, because he gets the status of children through Leah and the benefits of love and companionship through Rachel.

But, in the end, does Jacob really win? The plaintive plea of his beloved wife, "Give me children or I will die," is answered. Rachel gives birth to Joseph, and names him "God has added" in the expectation of having more. But it is not to be. She dies in childbirth with Benjamin. Jacob loses in the end, when his dear Rachel dies early. Leah, the unloved one, is buried next to Jacob in the Cave of Machpela. She lies next to him in the family plot, while Rachel is buried on the road. Though not his companion in life, Leah is his companion in death.

The denouement of the story comes in the next generation. Leah's sons will grow to hate and envy Rachel's son Joseph. We expect a replay of the family history. But Joseph triumphs over their hate, and finally, we get our happy ending. When the brothers all reconcile in Egypt many years later, after both Leah and Rachel have died, we can imagine the two women embracing, weeping, and reconciling too. Through the children they both wanted so much, the sisters can be sisters again.

The last word on Leah and Rachel is not in these chapters of Genesis. The last word is in the book of Leviticus, chapter 18, verse 18. Here it states that a man may not marry a woman and her sister. We have learned our lesson. It is not worth the aggravation. Traditionally, male commentators have understood the aggravation from their own perspective. Why have two women fighting over you all the time? But Leah and Rachel never annoyed Jacob with petty fighting or jealous competition. In truth, it was not worth the aggravation for the *sisters*. Sisters will not be compromised again for the sake of a man.

The Women of the Exodus Story: A Study in Community

> Rabbi Avera said, "Because of the righteousness of that generation of women, all Israel was redeemed from Egypt . . . and when the Holy One was revealed at the Sea, they were the first to recognize it and said, 'This is My God!' (Sotah 11b)

The story of Israelite slavery and subsequent freedom is the centerpiece of the Torah. Here Israelite identity is formed; from a tribe, to a band of slaves, to a people. Before the book of Exodus we have stories of heroes and heroines, who, though human, represent our more ancient mythological beginnings. With the story of Moses, the Torah becomes our history, whose climax is known: the giving of the law at Sinai. The story of Egypt is crucial not only because of its critique of slavery, but because of its positive and moralistic ending. Once bonded to Pharaoh, we are now bonded to God. Once servants to humans, we become servants to God.

There is no freedom from rules or rulership at Sinai. However, the locus of those rules has changed from human hands to the Mighty Arm of God. If we find spirituality in Exodus, it is a rule-based spirituality: Meet Me at the Holy Mountain and bind yourself to Me as once you were bound to Pharaoh. You will be in relationship to God when you follow God's rules.

From a sociological perspective, one could analyze this grand theme of Exodus by using Carole Gilligan's model of the development of girls and boys.[24] Boys, her studies suggest, develop a view of the world as a series of rules. Girls develop a view of the world as a series of relationships. The men of the Exodus story follow the rules, with the notable exception of the episode of the Golden Calf. The women work secretly against the rules, in favor of the value of human relationships. The men accept the rules at Sinai and get a reward: the priesthood, the land, tribal heads. But it is the women who keep the system running through their empathy and compassion.

We see this empathy in the introductory Exodus narrative, which precedes Moses' birth and highlights the two women who made his and other births possible: the midwives who refused to throw Hebrew baby boys into the Nile.

Pharaoh commands that the boys are to be killed, the girls left alive. In a male-centered polygamous society, girls are sexually useful as future wives and concubines. Boys as future enemy soldiers pose a clearer threat. As sons of an enslaved population, they wait to fill their roles as future rebels. Yet Pharaoh didn't understand that women bonding together against him might provide a different, unexpected rebellion.

Shifra and Puah

> The king of Egypt spoke to the Hebrew midwives, one of whom was named Shifrah and the other Puah, saying, "When you deliver the Hebrew women, look at the birthstool—if it is a boy, kill him; if it is a

girl, let her live." The midwives, fearing God, did not do as the king of Egypt had told them. (Exodus 1:15–17)

One would expect the book of Exodus to begin with the birth of Moses. It does not. It begins with a brief historical note to put the story in context, stating that the new king of Egypt did not know Joseph. The new regime forgot, or more likely changed, the lenient, pro-Israelite stance of the old regime. After this note, the first important characters we meet are the midwives Shifra and Puah. Apparently both midwifery and the use of a birthstool (literally "two stones," on which birthing women would sit or squat to deliver the baby, with the midwife "catching" the newborn underneath) were common enough for the Torah to note them without further explanation. It seems women were trained in this profession, medically able, and available; in some sense, independent workers. Only two midwives for the whole female population seems inadequate. Perhaps, then, these two were the overseers of a whole guild of midwives, or themselves heads of teams of women.[25] And while we do not ever learn the name of the monarch—he is simply called "Pharaoh" or "the king of Egypt"—we immediately know the names of these two women, Shifra and Puah. Seven times the word "midwives" is used, further attesting to their pivotal role. If the book of Exodus intended to glorify Moses, it would begin with him. Instead, the book begins by deliberately introducing the centrality of moral defiance to oppression through these two women who were common people of uncommon valor.

Who were Shifra and Puah? The Hebrew is ambiguous; the English translation misleading. It is not clear whether or not they were "Hebrew midwives" or rather "midwives to the Hebrews."

Miyaldot ha-ivriot can mean two things: "The midwives *who are* Hebrews" or "the midwives *to* the Hebrews." It would be odd for Pharaoh to expect Hebrews to kill their own babies (as if any midwives could kill *any* baby they deliver!). If they are indeed Hebrews, they have achieved some personal status among slaves, or perhaps, just as girls were spared from the Nile but boys killed, women were spared from slavery and men enslaved.

If they are Hebrews, they exhibit extraordinary defiance against the Pharaoh. If they are Egyptians, their bravery is even more remarkable. They hold enough importance for Pharaoh to command them directly by speech—or perhaps they pose enough of a threat. They belong to the privileged class, to be rewarded handsomely for doing Pharaoh's dirty work. Thus they stand to lose a great deal if they aid the Hebrew women, who belong to the slave caste. Shifra and Puah give us a glimpse of a female "underground railroad." They "fear God." They are more afraid of God than of Pharaoh. If they are not Hebrews, whose God do they fear—their own or the God of the Hebrews? By coming into contact with Hebrew women, they are influenced by the monotheism and loyalty they witness and are inspired to fear the Hebrew God. They respect how much the Hebrew women have retained their dignity. Shifra and Puah do not accept this tyranny over the Hebrews by the new regime, for perhaps they remember the "old days" when Hebrews and Egyptians lived together in peace. Either way, they teach us a lesson in civil disobedience.

When Pharaoh tests them and asks why the Hebrew boys are not being killed, they avoid the truth by placing the onus on the Hebrew women. "Because the Hebrew women are not like the Egyptian women: they are vigorous [in Hebrew *chayot*, literally, wild animals.] Before the midwife can come to them, they have given birth." They placate Pharaoh; they give the answer Pharaoh wants, seemingly sarcastic and denigrating. "Those Hebrew women are like wild animals." He cannot contradict them, since in this realm he has no expertise, knowledge or experience. The midwives prevail.

> And God dealt well with the midwives; and the people multiplied and increased greatly. And because the midwives feared God, He established households for them. (Exodus 1: 20–21)

This is once again the traditional, Jewish way of looking at the world: *middah k'neged middah*—for every kindness, you are paid back by the same kindness. What goes around comes around. God deals well with the midwives and multiplies the people. The legacy of the midwives to the Hebrews is a fitting one. The Hebrews survive and multiply and have more babies. And for themselves—as they saved children, so were they blessed with children.

Now the Pharaoh must acknowledge his failure to enlist the midwives in his program of destruction. He charges *all* the people, in Exodus 1: 22, to take over the task of death.

The lessons of the midwives are very potent ones. They teach us that there are people who can be trusted among all groups. In our Torah, whose mandate is to tell of our enslavement by the Egyptians and invalidate their evil ways, we meet these two authentically human women who do good. If they are Egyptians, then within the story of the enemy they teach us that there are no stereotypes, and that in every crisis also lies the opportunity to lift yourself above that crisis. In times of oppression, opportunities arise to overcome oppression. They use intelligence against force. The Pharaoh makes decrees about people he does not see. These women do not live in the palace. They assist with births every day, seeing true life and death. They function in the realm of real people every day. While Pharaoh decrees life and death high up in the palace, these women deliver it below, on earth. The birth of the Jewish people at Sinai owes much to these two birth helpers.

Yocheved, Pharaoh's daughter, and Miriam

> A certain man of the house of Levi went and married a Levite woman. The woman conceived and bore a son, and when she saw how beautiful he was, she hid him for three months. (Exodus 2:1–2)

When we first meet Moses' parents, they are unnamed. The Torah avoids any identification of the birth of our hero with supernatural miracles or superhumans. No virgin mother, no gargantuan father. He is born, hidden and retrieved by very earthly, normal characters—all of whom are female. The text saves the miracles for later, at the Sea, at Sinai, marvels to be performed not by humans, but by God. Moses will be the savior of the Jewish people when he is called by God as an adult to go to Pharaoh and "let My people go." But for now, he is simply a Hebrew baby, anonymous, unnamed and in danger.

Later, in Exodus 6: 20, his parents are identified. His father is called Amram; his mother, actually Amram's aunt (apparently such a marriage was still allowed), is named Yocheved.

This reference in Exodus 6:20 is the only place in the Torah where the name of Moses' mother is mentioned. Her name suggests humility: *Ya-kavod*, to God the glory goes. Not to me, the mother, but to the Father (God-*Yah* in Hebrew.) The human father, Amram, is completely peripheral in the story, overshadowed by Yocheved and Miriam. He plays no role in the hiding or subsequent saving of his child.

> And the woman conceived and bore a son; when she saw that he was a beautiful child, she hid him three months. When she could hide him no longer, she got a wicker basket [literally: ark] for him and caulked it with bitumen and pitch. She put the child in it and placed it among the reeds by the bank of the Nile. And his sister stationed herself at a distance, to learn what would befall him. (Exodus 2: 2–4)

Why could she hide him no longer? According to Rashi, it was easy to hide him for three months, because during Yocheved's first trimester she did not show. Only when she began to show would the Egyptians know she was pregnant and begin to expect and count down the days for the baby. Since they would begin counting her nine months of pregnancy from her first month of showing, they would actually come up three months short. After the baby's birth, she could hide him for three months, since the Egyptians did not figure she had given birth yet.

Three months after his birth, the child is placed in a basket in the water by the reeds, prefiguring the Sea of Reeds where Israel would later be saved. There is only one other instance in the Torah of the word *tevah* (basket). It is also used for the ark that Noah built to save the animals and his family from the flood. There, just as a few "chosen" were saved through Noah in a *tevah*, here will all the "chosen" be saved through a baby in a *tevah*.

Would a mother hide only a "beautiful" child? *Tov* can be translated as "good," meaning either "healthy" or "quiet." She knew he could survive in the basket if he was healthy, and if he was quiet. Many new mothers remark on their placid, docile babies as being "good" babies. His docility would make it easier for him to survive.

When we first meet Miriam, she, like her parents, is unnamed. She is referred to simply as "his sister." The midrash suggests that from this story of waiting and watching at the shore, she gets her later title of "prophet" (Exodus 15: 20)—one who is able to stand afar and see what will happen.[26] Miriam plays a crucial role in the Exodus story. She organizes Moses' adoption by the Pharaoh's daughter. She ensures that Moses is brought back to his mother for nursing. And later she leads the women in song and dance at the sea.

In Micah 6, we read of the "team" of three leaders: Miriam, Aaron and Moses. In the Talmud we read, "Three good leaders arose for Israel: Miriam, Moses and Aaron. On their account, three things were given to the Israelites, the well, the pillar of smoke and the manna."

Miriam becomes associated with the ability of the Israelites to find water in the desert. Almost every story in which she appears takes place near water. "All the time that Miriam was with them, a well of water followed them. When she died, the well dried up, and there was no water. That is why it says, 'And she died' and in the very next verse it says, 'And there was no water.'"[27]

> The daughter of Pharaoh came down to bathe in the Nile, while her maidens walked along the Nile. She spied the basket among the reeds and sent her slavegirl to fetch it. When she opened it, she saw that it was a child, a boy crying. She took pity on it and said, "This must be a Hebrew child." Then his sister said to Pharaoh's daughter, "Shall I go and get a Hebrew nurse to suckle the child for you?" And Pharaoh's daughter answered, "Yes," and the girl went and called the child's mother. And Pharaoh's daughter said to her, "Take this child and nurse it for me, and I will pay your wages." So the woman took the child and nursed it. (Exodus 2: 5–9)

Did Pharaoh's daughter really not know the identity of the child? Did she not realize that the Hebrew nurse was the child's own mother? It changes the tone of the story if she did indeed know more than she let on at the Nile that day. Perhaps she and Miriam and Yocheved were all working together. Why else would she offer to pay wages to a slave woman? She has great mercy, not only on the child, but on the whole family. She takes in the infant, and financially and materially aids the family by paying Yocheved to be her own child's wet nurse. As royalty, she has no reason to pay this Hebrew slave. As a woman, she has compassion on another woman.

I picture her as an unmarried woman who longs for a child of her own. She meets Yocheved's eyes and they understand each other. Pharaoh's daughter—the daughter of the enemy—is presented in a very positive light. She pities a Hebrew child, a child her father has ordered to be killed. She takes a risk by bringing this Hebrew child into the palace—the palace of the man who has ordered the child killed—to be raised as her own son. Surely this is a most independent woman, unafraid of her powerful father!

According to biblical scholar Nahum Sarna, "that the princess can personally execute such a contract accords with the relatively high social and legal position of women in Egypt. She possessed rights of inheritance and disposal of property, and she enjoyed a fair measure of economic independence."[28] She seeks no permission from her father to take the baby. Does she have a home or even a palace of her own where his orders will not reach? Imagine her as part of an early insurrection against her own father, knowing that taking in a Hebrew boy would be the ultimate act of rebellion.

And why did she go to the Nile on just that day? The midrash suggests she was going to it as a mikveh, to rid herself of the impurities of her father's house.[29] She is righteous, more righteous than Pharaoh, and worthy to be the "adoptive" mother of the man who will eventually overturn her father's kingdom. Perhaps she secretly hopes for just such an outcome.

> Then Miriam the prophetess, Aaron's sister, took a timbrel in her hand and all the women went out after her in dance with timbrels. And Miriam chanted for them, "Sing to the Lord . . ." (Exodus 15: 20–21)

A great miracle: 600,000 Israelites walk through a sea, the water forming walls on either side. They safely arrive on the other shore, then the same waters drown the approaching enemy camp. Moses sings; Miriam dances.

Here the text identifies Miriam as Aaron's sister and not Moses' sister. This could indicate the presence of an anti-Moses "Miriam" faction. Remember, Aaron and Miriam together approach Moses later with the complaint "Has God spoken only through Moses? Has God not spoken through us as well?" in Numbers 12. In other words, they ask, "Are we not also prophets?" They felt equal as leaders to Moses. They resented his centrality and their marginalization. Miriam is punished in that episode with leprosy for her insolence, but Aaron receives no retribution at the time. Miriam, the rebellious leader ever since her part at the splitting of the sea, seems to be viewed as the greater threat.

The Torah tells us that Moses had a speech impediment, and that Aaron would be his mouthpiece in Egypt, to speak for him to Pharaoh. Here, at the sea, Miriam is Moses' mouthpiece, to speak for him to the women. The men sing a song of military victory, but the women dance. They dance with instruments, with joy and gladness. Miriam is a musician; the text indicates no discomfort with women as musicians and dancers.

The children must have been frightened by what they have witnessed. What do women do when children are scared? They sing, they clap their hands, they dance. It is not coincidental that is the women, not the men, who take up instruments for dancing.

We can also imagine that the women were used to singing. Maybe they had sung together in Egypt to ease the burden of their husbands and friends. When they left Egypt, the women took what was most important to them, what was part of women's culture: the tambourines, their music. As in other Near Eastern tribes, it is possible that women were professionalized as guilds of keeners, funeral singers, ceremonial musicians.

Miriam repeats the refrain of Moses' song. This appears to be an antiphony, the men singing once, the women answering. Did Miriam lead only the women? The Hebrew in verse 21 reads *v'tan lahem*. *Lahem* can mean "them," masculine plural, or masculine and feminine plural, but very rarely would it be used only for women; in that case it would be written *lehen*. Based on the grammar, Miriam is singing here for both men and women, not only for women as is traditionally understood. She plays a central role. Perhaps she is the first female cantor!

The unit now closes: Miriam once stood as a child to see from afar what would happen to her baby brother as he was placed in the Nile. Now she stands as a woman, a leader, again from afar—on the other side of the Nile this time—and leads a thankful throng.

These women of the Exodus story—the midwives, Pharaoh's daughter, Yocheved and Miriam—are in rebellion, acting together against Pharaoh. They are collaborators, women acting as a counter-cultural force, against Pharaoh's oppression, negating it any way they can. Yes, even his own daughter! The women in the story are anti-establishment, if the establishment is Pharaoh. That is a powerful message not only for Passover, for which this story is so central, but for all human liberation. These women do not act "behind the scenes"—they actively affect history.

Tzipporah

> Now the priest of Midian had seven daughters. They came to draw water, and filled the troughs to water their father's flock, but shepherds came and drove them off. Moses rose to their defence, and he watered their flock. When they returned to their father Reuel, he said, "How is it that you have come back so soon today?" They answered, "An Egyptian rescued us from the shepherds; he even drew water for us and watered the flock." He said to his daughters, "Where is he then? Why did you leave the man? Ask him in to break bread." Moses consented to stay with the man, and he gave Moses his daughter Tzipporah as wife. (Exodus 2: 16–21)

The daughter of a foreign priest seems an unlikely candidate for Moses' wife! Yet he meets her at a well: echoes of all the matriarchs who meet their husbands at the well. The priest's daughters come to draw water, and there meet the man whose name means "drawn from the water." He protects the women from the male harassment which was likely a normal occurrence at a spot so identified with young, marriageable women.

Given by her father, almost as a "prize" for his help at the well, Tzipporah quickly becomes a pivotal character when she saves Moses' life in Exodus 4. In this strange narrative, Moses—or his son, it is not clear which—is in terrible danger.

> At a night encampment on the way, the Lord encountered him and sought to kill him. So Tzipporah took a flint and cut off her son's foreskin, and touched his legs with it, saying, "You are truly a bridegroom of blood to me!" And when God let him alone, she added, "A bridegroom of blood because of the circumcision." (Exodus 4: 24–26)

Familiar with circumcision from her Midianite culture, Tzipporah takes control of the situation. Perhaps she thinks God is angry with Moses for neglecting to circumcise their son while they were in Egypt. She is aware of the danger of the Israelite God's wrath on those who are "cut off," separated from their people because of some inaction or failure to obey. Their son, Gershom, may very well be "cut off," for his name means "I was a stranger there." Where is "there?" Either Moses felt estranged in Egypt, or in Midian, or never felt at home among the Israelites. Moses and his family are ultimately strangers, wherever "there" happens to be.

Only a few verses earlier God promises Moses that the firstborn sons of Egypt will be destroyed, but God's own firstborn son, Israel, will be saved. The sign of that deliverance will be the blood of the pascal sacrifice on the lintels of Israelite houses. The blood of Moses' firstborn, through circumcision, is needed to begin that process. For if Gershom remains uncircumcised, he remains an Egyptian until he is brought into the Israelite covenant. How can he be saved in Egypt without being circumcised, brought into the Israelite tribe, the tribe to be rescued? How can he be passed over with the rest of the firstborn of Israel? God has already prophesied!

Tzipporah touches his legs, a euphemism for his genitals, and a symbol of the two doorposts upon which the blood of deliverance must later be painted. She daubs him with the blood of deliverance. The same verb is used here as in Exodus 12: 22, when the Israelites "touched" blood on their doors.

The circumcision was, in a metaphorical way, a sacrifice. Nahum Sarna suggests that although the specific meaning of Tzipporah's action remains a mystery, the elements of the story suggest ritual-sacrificial significance.[30] Tzipporah acts in a way reminiscent of male priests who sprinkle and dash blood, which is not surprising, given her own lineage as the daughter of a Midianite priest. Perhaps she had the status of a Midianite priestess as well. Her quick and decisive action saves the hero's life and allows the family to continue on to Egypt, where Moses can begin the work of liberation. Her act clearly pleases God, for her husband's and son's lives are no longer in danger. She is the first female mohel.

All the women of the Exodus story, except Pharaoh's daughter, are named: Shifra and Puah, Yocheved, Miriam, Tzipporah. They all, in one way or another, save Moses' life and make the Exodus possible. They teach of women's strength in numbers, of women's ability to organize and cooperate, of the power of women's will and the ability to change history. They are powerful in their own context, and remain powerful in ours. These women choose conscious action, despite inherent dangers. They reject Pharaoh's dominion and resist his life-threatening decrees. In doing so they reject, as best they can, patriarchy and the death, warfare, disease and devaluing of personhood that results from it. They challenge the system even while living in it, with it and despite it.

The Daughters of Tzelophehad

> The daughters of Tzelophehad, of Manassite family—son of Heber son of Gilead son of Machir son of Manasseh son of Joseph—came forward. The names of the daughters were Machlah, Noah, Hoglah, Milcah and Tirtzah. They stood before Moses, Eleazar the priest, the chieftains and the whole assembly, at the entrance of the Tent of Meeting, and they said, "Our father died in the wilderness. He was not one of the faction, Korach's faction, which banded together against the Lord, but died for his own sin; and he has left no sons. Let not our father's name be lost to his clan just because he had no sons! Give us a holding among our father's kin!" Moses brought the case before the Lord. And the Lord said to Moses, "The plea of Tzelophehad's daughters is just. You should give them a hereditary holding among their father's kin. Transfer their father's share to them. Further, speak to the Israelite people as follows: If a man dies without leaving a son, you shall transfer his property to his daughter . . ." (Numbers 27: 1–8)

The book of Numbers opens with a census of adult males who are able to bear arms, listed by clans of ancestral houses. This census is repeated in Chapter 26. The listing of Israelites by clan is extremely important, because the ownership of land will be determined by it; the basis for land distribution in the newly conquered Israel will be those ancestral houses. In this context, the daughters of Tzelophehad reveal a significant new piece of information: that the elders have not yet decided what the role of women would be in that land distribution. This is also an important story because it shows the potential for variation from the strictly patriarchal society of biblical times.

Contingencies such as clans without sons have not yet come

up, or have not yet been dealt with legally. The daughters must plead their case as a new one. There seems to be no precedent with which Moses can answer them. The story of Tzelophehad's daughters is the only case in which the law is not precise about the role of women in the tribal infrastructure.

All five daughters, Machlah, Noah, Hoglah, Milcah and Tirtza, are immediately named, and their "good" ancestry through Joseph is established. They speak as one, stating their case briefly and succinctly. It is evident that the daughters know that, according to the laws set out in Chapter 26, no one from their father's family will receive a portion in the land. They plead their cause with that knowledge.

They begin with a personal statement, about their father and his death. It is a ingenious way to start their speech, making it clear that they are not in opposition to Moses. Their father was not a member of the rebellious Korach faction. These five women do not appear to be threatening to the system; they care only in a personal way. They do not argue for all women to inherit, just themselves. They end together with a clear and passionate demand, with no equivocation: "Give us a holding among our father's kin!" From this entreaty, the midrash compares the intense desire of the women to be in the land with the reluctance of the men to enter it.[31]

Moses seems stymied. The reader expects to hear an answer from him, reiterating the already established law. The elders say nothing. The case goes directly to the highest authority: to God. Moses knows this is a "hot issue." We can imagine that women have grumbled about this before, have questioned their role in land distribution, ever since the census counted them out. Some of those now joined with the Israelites in the desert come from cultures in which women had the right to inherit, and they feel cheated. The daughters probably know of earlier, more ancient Near Eastern legal practices which did on occasion allow daughters to inherit when there was no son, and therefore they specified that their father had left no sons.[32] Even though the daughters of Tzelophehad petition only for themselves, Moses hears in their protest the voices of other women, and does not want to answer the challenge himself.

God's answer is also brief and direct. The daughters of Tzelophehad are right. Give them their share. The result of their plea, whether they hoped for it or not, whether they planned for it or not, has ramifications for all women. All daughters may now inherit when there is no son.

The challenge to authority that comes from these women is extraordinary. It is noteworthy that they are individually named, unlike many other women in the Bible. They come as single women, unattached to men. They face the entire leadership, and they gather in public at the Tent of Meeting. Five unmarried women change Israelite law and history by opposing the injustice of patriarchy. That a patriarchal document would include this story is not only remarkable, but also attests that the document somehow acknowledges the justice of the opposition. Unlike Korach's followers the daughters are not punished for their rebellion, even though they questioned Moses and the elders and their control. The earth does not open up and swallow them for their impudence. Instead, God comes to their aid and says for all generations to hear: they are right. But the story does not end there.

> The family heads in the clan of the descendants of Gilead son of Machir son of Manasseh, one of the Josephite clans, came forward and appealed to Moses and the chieftains, family heads of the Israelites.

> They said, "The Lord commanded my lord to assign the land to the Israelites as shares by lot, and my lord was further commanded by the Lord to assign the share of our kinsman Tzelophehad to his daughters. Now if they marry persons from another Israelite tribe, their share will be cut off from our ancestral portion and be added to the portion of the tribe into which they marry; thus our allotted portion will be diminished . . ." So Moses, at the Lord's bidding, instructed the Israelites, saying, "The plea of the Josephite tribe is just. This is what the Lord has commanded concerning the daughters of Tzelophehad: They may marry anyone they wish, provided they marry into a clan of their father's tribe . . . Every daughter among the Israelite tribes who inherits a share must marry someone from a clan of her father's tribe, in order that every Israelite may keep his ancestral share . . ." The daughters of Tzelophehad did as the Lord had commanded Moses: Machlah, Tirtzah, Hoglah, Milcah and Noah, Tzelophehad's daughters, were married to the sons of their uncles, marrying into the clans of descendants of Manasseh son of Joseph; and so their share remained in the tribe of their father's clan. (Numbers 36: 1–3, 5–6, 8, 10–12)

Now we see the repercussions of the daughters' challenge. They take action for the sake of their father's name; their father's name must be guarded. The men of the tribe suddenly wonder what this new freedom of inheritance for all women will mean. Individually unnamed, as a group, the men appeal the rights given to the daughters of Tzelophehad in Numbers 27 in front of a smaller leadership cadre this time, and not at the central Tent of Meeting. The daughters themselves—or any women, for that matter—are not present to comment or refute.

Moses brings God's answer, but does not query God first. The reader wonders what part Moses himself may have played in the second decision, for we do not hear him bring the case directly to God. We note that the wording is exactly the same in Moses' answer: The plea of the Josephite tribe is just; as the plea of Tzelophehad's daughters was just. Both sides must be placated.

The men of the tribe present a personal gripe that is troubling to them alone, but it does not remain an individual gripe. Like the case of the daughters, the individual case is generalized for all women. First freedom is given, then it is curtailed.

The daughters do as they are told, and they marry from their father's clan. We could say they do not win in the end, since their choice of mates is curtailed. Yet that is not so, since in the closed Hebrew marital system the most desirable mate *is* from within your own clan anyway. While at the end, the freedom of women is restricted by this second proclamation, women get a role and a place within the inheritance structure of Israel, and their voices have been heard. The daughters of Tzelophehad critique an injustice and God listens. The Torah records a change within its own structure for the benefit of women, and, in the end, the words remain clear in our ears as God spoke them first: The daughters are right. When they win, all women win. This tale must have had a place in the hearts of those who heard it, and an emotional tug on listeners long ago.

The rabbis of the Talmud extol the virtues of these women in the midrash. "It was taught: The daughters of Tzelophehad were wise women, they were interpreters, and they were virtuous. They must have been wise, since they spoke at an opportune time . . . They must have been interpreters, for they said, 'If he had a son, we would not have spoken' . . . They must have been virtuous, since they were married only to men worthy of them."[33]

Furthermore, it troubled the rabbis that the daughters of

Tzelophehad were expected to marry only from their father's tribe, and they "fixed" it with a midrash. Rav Judah said in the name of Rav Samuel:

> The daughters of Tzelophehad were given permission to be married to any of the tribes, as it is said [in Numbers 36: 6], "Let them be married to whom they want . . ." How then do you explain the rest of the verse following, "Only let them marry into the tribe of their father?" Scripture was giving them good advice, that is, that they should be married only to those worthy of them, namely, their family.[34]

So they did marry whom they wanted; they just chose to marry whom they wanted within the allowable system. The daughters of Tzelophehad challenged the system outright, forcefully and honestly, while living within it. They are a kind of early prototype of the Jewish feminist today who critiques Judaism first for herself, then for other women, and then remains in it to see its faults corrected. These five women are the activists of their time, rewarded for their personal social conscience with a better society for everyone.

PART II

Blood and Water: The Stuff of Life

When I passed by you and saw you
wallowing in your blood,
I said to you, "In your blood, live!
Ezekiel 16: 6

A prayer:
some day, some month
perhaps this month
let my body and its blood
at long last teach me the lesson
I struggle so against accepting
let go let go let go give up control
surrender to the flow of life within.

Merle Feld

Introduction

Christian theologian and teacher Elizabeth Dodson Gray succinctly noted, "Women's bodies may be the hardest place for women to find sacredness."[35] We instinctively know that. Our bodies are demeaned by the media, used to sell products from cars to screwdrivers and objectified in pornography. With our feet bound, clitorises cut or sewn for greater male enjoyment, we are still too tall, too fat, never just right. For many years male medical practitioners told us how we should feel, and "cured" us of everything, including female physical ailments such as "hysteria."

Today our reaction to our own menstruation and menopause is carefully studied, documented and then decoded—mostly by men. Predominantly male chemists invent new medicines to take care of our female problems. We even have a "proven" malaise that once a month can cause us to become irrational ax-murderers: PMS, premenstrual syndrome. With all this bad press, how are we supposed to see God's wondrous work within us?

Instinctively, we know that we are sexual, sensuous creatures, but this sexuality has been carefully legislated by most religions. Our sexuality has been bifurcated between the "good girl" (modest, long sleeves, quiet voice) and the "bad girl" (shorts, tight top, loud voice). "Good" girls follow the rules. They don't socialize much with men until they are dutifully married. They don't question their place in the pecking order and don't rock the boat. "Bad" girls tempt men with their raw sensuousness; they laugh too loud; they drink and flirt. They are usually iconoclasts and question authority. Bad girls use their bodies to attract men. Good girls ignore their bodies. With this dichotomy, how can we affirm our bodies in a spiritual way?

Judaism posits a healthy sexuality for both men and women. Put simply, sex is not considered "dirty," only regulated to certain times, certain places, and with certain people. With those parameters maintained, sex is a holy act. With those parameters broken, sex is not. Those parameters require sex to be pleasurable for both the man and the woman. Within a heterosexual marriage, almost any kind of lovemaking is permitted to achieve that pleasure. A husband's marital responsibility includes his wife's sexual pleasure, so much so that a traditional marriage certificate, the *ketubah*, stipulates that the wife may expect regular and enjoyable sexual activity. Force is never permitted; Judaism recognizes the existence of marital rape and deems it abhorrent.[36]

All this points to the possibility of a healthy female sexuality in a Jewish context. If we learn to revalue our bodies as an intrinsic part of our souls, and reject the inherited Western/Christian split between mind and body, we can also reevaluate what it would mean to have rituals that acknowledge women's sexuality.

In Part II of this book, we explore women as physical beings in the Torah. We examine whether the Torah gives mixed messages when dealing with the physical realities of women's bodies. Why do the terms "purity" and "impurity" play such a large role in the Torah's restrictions around women?

Blood and water are the stuff of birth, the physical stuff of life, and both are connected to women. Both can symbolize life or death, birth or destruction. Females bleed predictably and cyclically once a month for most of their adult life, yet they do not die. Females break a sac of water which flows out of them, yet they do not die. In blood and water we give life, and except in rare cases, live ourselves.

Mary Douglas has written, "Why should bodily refuse be a symbol of danger and of power? . . . [A]ll margins are dangerous . . .

Spittle, blood, milk, urine, feces or tears by simply issuing forth have transversed the boundary of the body."[37]

All margins spell danger. The body, both the physical body and the communal body, that is, society, must have boundaries. Douglas suggests that the human body is a metaphor for society in all ways: its looseness is everyone's looseness, its borders everyone's borders. We look out beyond ourselves and see others like us. What happens to them happens to us. With the human body as metaphor, Judaism's obsession with boundaries becomes an obsession with human life as we know it. It is interesting to note that Judaism does not see spittle, milk, urine, feces or tears as crossing the boundaries, only blood and semen. The latter substance Douglas has left off her list. This is sexual stuff, the stuff of life and death, the symbol of danger and power. This is the matter of the human body, intersecting with the metaphors made by the human mind.

The Torah responds to these substances with what anthropologists call "taboos." Taboos are the system by which certain objects or persons are set aside as either sacred or accursed. Such objects or persons inspire both fear and respect.

Bodily taboos focus on the nexus points of life and death. In the Torah, those bodily taboos revolve around the emission of semen, blood, and the end of blood in the corpse. Through ejaculation, menstruation, childbirth and contact with a corpse, we see ourselves as dying and then living again. In the corpse's face we see our own. The man who ejaculates experiences the letting-go of self in a total way, being brought to the brink. A woman who gives birth may say she felt that she was in "the other world" at transition. The Torah restricts contact with semen and blood, the male and female stuff of life, acknowledging their mystery and power. It also restricts contact with those who, at certain different times, emit these substances. Although it does not explicitly say so, there is a sense of awe at the mystery and power not only of the substances themselves, but of the human beings who release them. Yet the Torah has no public celebrations acknowledging this mystery and power, nor acknowledging the first and last times females acquire it.

Water functions in the Torah as the place of purification from the taboos of semen and blood, and it too has both sanctifying and terrifying power. The *mikveh*, the pool of living waters into which the "dead" mix themselves, simulates an experience of drowning and then resurrection. About this experience at the *mikveh*, Aryeh Kaplan writes, "When a person immerses himself in water, he places himself in an environment where he cannot live. Were he to remain submerged for more than a few moments, he would die from lack of air . . . in a sense, the *mikveh* also represents the grave . . . The representation of the *mikveh* as both womb and grave is not a contradiction. Both are places of non-breathing, and are end points of the cycle of life."[38]

Jewish women today question the origins of the Torah's taboos around blood and water, and challenge the restrictions around female physicality. Feminists wonder if it is possible to wrest the mikveh from its historic associations and "re-vision" it as a new place of sanctity for women. No doubt the future will see a variety of feminist ceremonies that revolve around celebrating the link between women's physicality and sexuality.[39]

Blood and Its Symbolism in the Torah

As a woman who menstruates, I am fascinated by the tension in the Torah between blood as purifying and blood as defiling, a tension whose modern implications still resonate with me. Do I feel a partner in God's creation at this wondrous moment or do I hate being female, cursed and burdened with a bloody mess? As a rabbi, I can choose to teach about menstruation in a new feminist way, glorifying it as a sacred moment and a life-cycle event. Or I can question the traditional "biology is woman/woman is biology" that has been reappropriated by second-wave feminists, and reject such ritual as too anatomy-based and too woman-specific.[40] In the Torah, is our blood holy, is it defiling, or is it just plain blood?

Metaphors of mystery and power, contact and avoidance dominate the Torah's expressions around blood. Blood, which is to be avoided in the realms of eating and sex, is the same substance that atones for the community in the sacrificial cult and binds the individual male child to the Israelite covenant through circumcision. It would be easy, as a feminist, to dismiss this contact/avoidance as a fear of women's sexual power, a misunderstanding, or a primitive attempt at understanding female anatomy. It may indeed be all of these things. But the restrictions and boundaries around menstruation need to be seen in light of the entire biblical duality of blood as the core of both life and death.

This theme is common in the Torah: in every potent symbol is the double quality, the twin potential of birth and decay, purity and impurity. Every aspect of the bodily experience has the potential to sanctify, but also to pollute. That which we value most has the power to both elevate and hurt us. Money, sex, power, all the things we desire, have the potential to act equally as sources of goodness or sources of evil. This explains a great part of our ancestors' ambivalence toward blood. The life force which flows through us and sustains us can also kill us. And only women shed this remarkable substance every month, copiously it may seem, and do not die.

Even though, in medical terms, we know today that menstrual fluid is not actual blood, but uterine lining and mucus, our ancestors deemed it blood. In the Torah, blood functions in both the symbolic realm and the utilitarian, daily arena. Symbolically, our ancestors believed it was the container of the soul and the life-force of every living creature, while on a practical level they used it as the necessary tool in major sacrificial rites. They deeply respected and feared the life-and-death power of blood. They curtailed its overuse, and curbed the potential for its misuse.

> Every creature that lives shall be yours to eat; just as with the plants I give you these. Except that flesh with its life-blood you shall not eat. For your own life-blood I will exact retribution [or: I will require a reckoning] for beast as well as human I will exact it . . . (Genesis 9: 3–5)

> For the life of the flesh is in the blood, and I have assigned it to you for expiation for your lives upon the altar; it is the blood, acting as life, that effects expiation. (Leviticus 17: 11)

A Jew cannot consume blood for two reasons. The first is an existential argument, that "the life of the flesh is in the blood." Since blood is the life force, it is wrong to take both the life and its essence. Our ancestors worried about the continuity of all species, since we are allowed to take animal life for food. But God assures us that all animal life will never be destroyed, and the rainbow is set in the sky as a sign of that promise of perpetuity, not only for humans but also animals. Leaving the blood behind is then a human assurance that the partnership of perpetuity will be kept. While animals will be slaughtered for food, they will not be totally annihilated. The unconsumed blood is a symbol of that human promise to the animals.

The second is an ownership issue: that life force rightfully belongs to God, who gave it, and who will require it later in the ritual pouring out and dashing of sacrificial blood in the Tabernacle. Since it belongs to God, it must be consecrated back to God. Where the prohibition against the partaking of blood is reiterated in Deuteronomy 23, we are informed that consecrated male firstlings are to be eaten annually in a sacrificial rite, but their blood must be poured out like water. Eating and sacrifice are linked. Blood serves a purpose: expiation in the sacrificial rites. To eat it would deny its central function in the sacrificial system and trivialize its ritual importance. To eat it would take it from its legal owner and ultimate user, which is God.

Unlike the law of consuming the meat of sacrifices, which is restricted only to males in Leviticus 6: 22, the prohibition against consuming blood in Leviticus 7: 26 applies to everyone: males and females, Israelites and non-Israelites, priests and commoners, not only in the sacred precincts but in all dwellings. Some have seen in this a kind of proto-vegetarianism in ancient Israel.[41] Since the eating of meat is permitted, and life must be taken in order to eat meat, the Torah adds a serious caveat. A reckoning must be done for the blood of the taken animal.

The reckoning will appear later in the form of "sacred slaughter," that is, the system of animal sacrifice elaborated in the book of Leviticus. There, the meat is "consumed" by fire for God or ritually eaten by priests; the blood poured out for God. Sacrifice through the priestly system elevates plain slaughter—killing for food—into a religious act for God rather than for ourselves.

Herbert Chanan Brichto has observed,

> Whenever man [*sic*] takes an animal life for his own table he must take that life on God's table, the blood spilling on this "altar" symbolizing

> man's awareness that it is not on his own recognizance that he appropriates for himself a life which, as he is not able to create it, he may not freely take. To fail to use God's table in slaughter is characterized as "eating (/eating with) the blood." Such failure has the import that the slaughter remains illicit. [42]

Such slaughter is not "sacred slaughter," for blood has a specific purpose assigned by God: as the life force, it offers expiation not just for the animal life taken, but for a whole host of human behavior enumerated in Leviticus. The shedding of animal blood for eating—plain slaughter for human benefit—is placated or balanced by the act of sacred slaughter.

For the Hebrews, sacrificial blood is not nourishment for the gods, as in other ancient religions. God doesn't need that blood. We do. Neither is it human nourishment, to emulate animal vitality or symbolize immortality. Our ancestors lived in societies where eating blood had magical properties. Thus the prohibition against blood consumption in Leviticus 19: 26 is linked to other acts, like sorcery or witchcraft. Maimonides interpreted the verse in Leviticus 20: 4–5 that cautions "do not eat round the blood," as a warning to the Israelites not to imitate heathens who, while abhorring the actual drinking of blood, held a sacrificial meal where they sat *around* the blood bowl in order to dine and commune with spirits. He notes that the punishment "I will set my face against" is used only here and in relation to idolatry, linking the eating of blood to idolatrous practices.[43]

In the sacrificial system, blood plays a highly physical and visual role. Priests sprinkled it on the horns of the altar for cleansing and dedication, spread it on earlobes and toes for consecration of initiates, dashed it around the altar itself, painted it on doorposts as a sign. The blood itself is holy, and you must wash it in a sacred place, since it is improper for blood to be anywhere else but in the sacrificial area. It is regularly poured on the ground and covered with earth, moved away or hidden. Its power is manifest, for it purifies objects by its touch.

Blood saves both the collective and the individual. The lamb's blood smeared on the doorposts of the Israelites saved their firstborn from destruction on the night of the first Passover. Here, too, blood both sustains and endangers, for it is the medium of both plague and deliverance.

For the Egyptians, the very source of their life in the desert, the drinking water of the Nile, was ruined and rendered abhorrent. Surely this terrible menace to potable water terrorized them. For them, blood meant death. But for the Israelites, blood meant life. Commanded to slaughter a lamb, the Israelites first use its blood for the lintels, then eat it in a sacred family meal. They paint their doorposts with the blood, using a brush made from the hyssop, which later in Leviticus will be used in sacrificial practices. The blood on their houses became a sign both for God and for them that no plague would harm them on the night of the slaying of the Egyptian firstborn. That sign of special protection is tinged with the reminder of in Whose hands rests the ultimate power of life and death. As a collective people, we will be born or reborn into freedom with that blood, as all individual beings are born through blood. Drora O'Donnell Setel suggests this smearing the Israelites' doorways with blood was "... an image suggestive of the birth canal."[44]

Blood has other characteristics in the Torah. It "speaks" in the story of Cain and Abel (Genesis 4) and "avenges for the crime of murder" (Numbers 35). Blood sanctifies the people in the Yom Kippur ritual (Leviticus 14: 11–15), and sanctifies the altar (Leviticus 14: 18–19); yet it defiles the Tabernacle (Leviticus 15:

31) and defiles the whole land (Numbers 35: 34.) Blood can sanctify a male through *brit milah*, or defile a female through menstruation and childbirth.

Menstruation and the Laws of Niddah

> When any man has an issue discharging from his sexual organ, he is ritually impure . . . When one with a discharge becomes purified from the discharge, he shall count off seven days for the purification, wash his clothes, and bathe his body in "living water" and become ritually pure . . . (Leviticus 15: 2,13)

> When a man has an emission of semen, he shall bathe his whole body in water and remain ritually impure until the evening . . . When a woman has her discharge, it being blood from her body, she shall be considered a *niddah* [menstruant or "put away"] for seven days, and whoever touches her shall be ritually impure until the evening . . . if a man lies with her, her condition of *niddah* is upon him and he shall be ritually impure seven days, and any bedding upon which he lies is also impure. When a woman has had a discharge of blood for many days, not at the usual time of her menstruation [*niddah*], she shall be ritually impure as at the time of her *niddah*; as long as her discharge lasts, she shall be ritually impure . . . When she is pure from her discharge, she shall count off seven days, and after that, she is ritually pure. On the eighth day she shall take two turtledoves or two pigeons, and bring them to the priest at the entrance to the Tent of Meeting. The priest shall offer the one as a sin offering and the other as a burnt offering, and the priest shall make expiation on her behalf for her ritually impure discharge. (Leviticus 15: 16, 19, 24–25, 28–30)

The Torah is vitally concerned with repopulation. In that sphere, sexuality is the conduit for birth, and in the eyes of the Torah, sexual fluids need to be controlled in the same way that sexuality needs to be controlled. In Genesis, God brought order into the chaos of creation. In Leviticus, God brings order into the chaos of human sexual creativity. The original intention of the Torah was to call attention to the workings of our bodies as sexual beings and to help us navigate that tightrope of the nexus between fluids of death and fluids of life. Men and women stood equally on that tightrope. Our ancestors understood the highly charged power of the symbolism of both semen and menstrual blood. They were awed and disturbed by both of them equally.

Those who discharged either substance, or any other undescribed substance from their sexual organs, were rendered ritually impure, in Hebrew *tamey*. For women, ritually impurity through menstrual blood has a second, specific word, *niddah*. This word is used to describe both the impurity and the woman who has it. *Niddah* in its verb form means to shun, or put away; in the noun form it means menstruant. The menstruating woman is ostracized among men, though not among women and children. And men experiencing a bodily emission from their genitals were similarly ostracized.

The Torah categorizes emissions as either normal or abnormal. Things are not in order when substances come out of places when they should not, where they should not and how they should not. Male genital discharge is normal when semen is discharged through ejaculation. It is abnormal (called in Hebrew *zav*) when pus comes from the penis (perhaps a venereal discharge). A normal seminal discharge causes a condition of "impurity" that lasts for the duration of the day and is ended at nightfall by washing. An abnormal discharge causes seven days of added impurity and requires a sacrifice after the bathing. Similarly, female genital emissions can be either normal (through menstruation) or abnormal (called *zava*, blood or staining at times other than menstruation). A normal menstrual flow is considered to take seven days.

Thus, a man's normal discharge lasts one day; abnormal, seven. A woman's normal discharge lasts seven days; abnormal, also seven. To be fair, a woman's menstrual period is usually close to seven days, and certainly never one day. Both males and females who have a genital emission cause "contagion" and any person or object that touches them becomes impure. Only men must "wash" before offering their sacrifice, perhaps because men approached God directly with their sacrifice, whereas women approached indirectly, through a priest who offered it for them. Possibly the Torah does not mention women's immersion in water at the end of the purification period because such a rule was obvious and inferred from the practice of men.

It should be noted that the Hebrew words for these emissions and their consequences are not words that echo their English translations well. *Tamey*, normally translated as either impure or unclean, has nothing to do with dirt. *Tahor*, translated as clean or pure, is not about physical cleanliness. These are, rather, ritual states, which ascertain whether or not the person having an emission may approach the cultic center, that is, the Tabernacle. The menstrual flow, or semen, is never considered *physically* unclean in and of itself.

> When a woman at childbirth bears a male, she shall be ritually impure seven days; she shall be impure as at the time of *niddah* . . . She shall remain in a state of blood purification for thirty-three days . . . if she

> bears a female, she shall be ritually impure for two weeks as during *niddah*, and she shall remain in a state of blood purification for sixty-six days. (Leviticus 12: 2, 3–5)

The childbirth *niddah* rules are more perplexing. Of course, there can be no male parallel to giving birth. But a woman can give birth to a boy or to a girl. When a woman gives birth to a male child, she is *niddah* for seven days, exactly as with a normal discharge. She then remains *niddah* for an additional thirty-three days, days in which it is presumed she still has postpartum genital bleeding. If she gives birth to a girl, she is *niddah* for exactly double that amount of time.

Interpretations abound among the rabbis as to that doubling of postpartum impurity. Some suggest it was merely for physical reasons. It was a common medieval notion (still held by some today) that after the birth of a girl there is a longer period of bleeding. Others suggest that the postpartum time of impurity is extended because the newborn girl will, someday in the future, also bleed. The new mother then is impure for herself and also for her daughter. Or, the double period of time may reflect apprehension and anticipation about the infant daughter's potential fertility.

The Leviticus section on genital emissions ends with a warning, "You shall put the Israelites on guard against their uncleanliness, lest they die through their uncleanliness by defiling My Tabernacle which is among them." The purity not only of the body, but also of the communal body represented by the Tabernacle, is at stake. Since we are created in God's image, the human body reflects the Divinity within us, and the genitals the maximal symbol of our creative partnership with God.

The first command, to be fruitful and multiply, is impossible without the smooth functioning of the genitals. The genitals are

God's holy place in the human body; they embody future generations and the spark of holiness to reproduce. Any emissions of blood or semen, whether normal or abnormal, are seen as entering that state of reproductive partnership. If thwarted, as in the case of menstrual blood not "in season" or semen not in intercourse, that partnership is not fulfilled. We wash in fresh waters, symbol of returning life, and offer sacrifice in sadness. Seen in the context of a society that believes that every manifestation of God, whether human or animal, is first and foremost commanded to procreate, and in procreating is most like God, strictures around the body and its emissions are highly symbolic and also utilitarian.

A Jewish Feminist Reexamination of Menstruation

The challenge is: How can we reappropriate the Torah's menstrual sections from a feminist viewpoint?

When I first got my period, I came home and told my mother, and I did not know what to expect. Upon hearing the news, my mother explained that when she got her period, her mother slapped her hard, and said, "Welcome to the pain of being a woman." But she wouldn't do that to me, oh no, she was a modern woman. She kissed me, and then gave me a little slap, just for tradition's sake. I did not know then, and I still do not know, to which tradition she was referring, though I suspect that many young women of the 1940s and 1950s received such little slaps. That was the only celebration many of us got in honor of becoming women.

Through the years, I have had my ups and downs with this monthly cycle. I have had cramps or no cramps, felt blue, felt sensuous; I have felt impatient and wished it would be over. But I have never felt nothing. Menstruation has always been a sign for me: of my body working or "not working," of a miraculous inner system, of being female.

I go to the *mikveh* each month, not so I may be "kosher" for my husband—I'm no chicken product—but as a woman bidding farewell to a regular part of myself. I am a woman who needs some way to existentially experience and then bless special moments. I never feel physically or spiritually dirty during my cycle. I do, however, feel a need to realign myself, to rebalance my emotions and attentions, which have been different during those days. I pay attention to my cycle: its presence has been reassuring and its absence was the first sign—a most welcome and spiritual one—when I wanted to become pregnant.

Because I have learned to count the days and months by my own body, I have never understood why the Jewish tradition such an essential part of my being—does not have a blessing for this regular monthly event. Surely a religion which boasts of a positive view of the body, a religion which has a blessing for an activity as mundane as going to the bathroom, would have a way to sacralize such a significant occurrence! The male composers of the liturgy, living in a world where modesty was central and women's bodies were a mystery at best, were not able—or more likely, not willing—to imagine such a blessing. They simply never composed one. If they had, where would it be found—in the back of the prayerbook with other daily blessings? I sometimes wonder if we had such a blessing passed by mother to daughter, which has been lost. Have women always felt ambivalent about menstruation and thus never risen up to bless it, even in private, among themselves?

I cannot accept this neglect, and neither can my body, which is tied inexorably to my Jewish soul. I began searching for a *bracha* (blessing) for menstruation years ago in rabbinical school. The first time we menstruate definitely deserves a more spiritual response than a slap! And menopause, the final parting with what has been a monthly event for years, deserves its recognition too.

I thought to invent a new *bracha*, then I decided to reinvent an old one. There is a prayer in the traditional daily and Shabbat service that many women and men across the denominational spectrum find difficult and offensive. It is found in the morning blessings, and in the Orthodox prayerbook appears as "Blessed are You, Adonai our God, Ruler of the Universe, who has not made me a woman." (Women say "who has made me according to Your will.") Valiant attempts have been made to explain this as men's gratefulness for the commandments that are incumbent upon them which would not be incumbent upon them if they were women. Another explanation is that it is a prayer of gratitude for not having to go through the pain of childbirth.

But whatever the fanciful or homiletic interpretations, this blessing remains a huge spiritual obstacle. I decided to tackle this negative expression, appropriate it, and turn it around for women.

Each month, at the time I see I have gotten my period, I say, "*Baruch atah Adonai, eloheinu melech ha-olam, she'asani ishah*: Blessed are You, Adonai our God, Ruler of the World, who has made me a woman." It sets the mood for the rest of my month. It is always a revolutionary moment, too, this blessing of my menses/month, as I realize that the slightest change in wording, removing the *lo*, changing the negative "who has *not* made me a woman" into the positive "who has made me a woman," affirms my own holiness and sanctity in God's eyes *within* the context of menstruation, not in spite of it. Sometimes I change the traditional opening of *baruch atah* to the feminine grammatical *brucha at*, and sometimes I use an opening which says "Blessed is the Source of Life." But whenever I say the blessing, I wish my mother had thought of this kind of acknowledgement when I was twelve.[45]

Naomi Goldenberg writes about the split between mind and body in modern Western religious thought. In such thought body is bad and mind is good; God is symbolized as closer to mind, or soul, or essence. "Godliness" means soul and therefore goodness. The absence of godliness means carnality and therefore evil. This bifurcation, she argues, is a result of monotheism. She writes, ". . . belief in transcendent entities may well encourage the devaluation of physical life."[46]

But feminists, even monotheistic ones, can reject this mind/body bifurcation. In the realm of menstruation and birth women have the most potent possibility of seeing ourselves as *both* body and spirit, an integrated whole. Our bleeding bodies, our creating bodies become a gateway to our souls. Our souls become a mirror of our bodies. We must hope it is possible to rescue the aspects of mystery inherent in menstruation. We can fully acknowledge the fearful elements of our being, being conscious of ourselves. Erich Neumann noted women in ancient times were conscious of themselves as the "subject and object of mysterious processes and as a vessel of transformation." Seeing ourselves as we menstruate as "vessels of transformation" would undoubtedly change the aura of self-negation we have inherited.

We can emerge from this discussion with a sense of the *mysterium tremendum* of life and death, which is in our own corporeal female selves, if we speak in completely different terms. Let us not say we are clean or unclean; we are instead "in a time of power" or "finished with the time of power." Sometimes I think of menstruation as a time of intense electrical charges—the charge of life and death—pulsing through my body. If you come too near such charges, they will hurt you. I need space and time to "neutralize" myself.

Though most of us would reject the menstrual huts of old, where women were sequestered until their menstrual period had passed, perhaps there is still some positive expression of separation we can reappropriate. A most eloquent argument for a positive identification of female blood with power is made by Penelope Washbourn in her article "Becoming Woman: Menstruation as Spiritual Challenge." She terms menstruation a "crisis in self identity" for a young girl. Cultures that allow the girl to experience this time of physical and emotional change as one of upheaval help her perceive female sexuality gracefully. Those like our own that ignore the crisis aspect of menstruation, increase women's anxiety rather than decrease it.

Washbourne writes:

> Menstruation symbolizes the advent of a new power that is mana or "sacred." A sacred power has life-giving and life-destroying possibilities, and in no case is mana to be taken lightly. A *taboo* expresses this feeling that something special, some holy power, is involved, and our response to it must be very careful. Even those societies which appear to have only negative attitudes toward menstruation—that is, place many restrictive taboos on the menstruating female and the community, are expressing a deep understanding of the essential sacredness of the event and of the need to ensure the beneficial effects of this sacred power.[47]

How should we deal with the notion that the *niddah* is to be "put away," far from men, only among other women? Washbourn suggests that seclusion, far from being oppressive, has an elevating aspect to it.

> Another element of menstrual taboos that is frequently ignored is the

> real need of the girl to withdraw psychologically and physically into solitude or into the presence of other women . . . The girl must wrestle with the meaning of her female identity, and withdrawal may have a positive function.[48]

We have lost the positive elements of being away from men. If we were to choose such seclusion voluntarily, and share our inner being, our sense of physical and spiritual power, and that "electrical charge" at menstruation time with other women, the older historical association with "menstrual huts" in some new, feminist form might be reappropriated.

Anthropologists and historians of ancient societies suggest that such menstrual separation was not always a negative experience. Monthly segregation in ancient societies was, as Erich Neumann suggests, a "movement of women into a sacred female precinct." He writes,

> The mysterious occurrence of menstruation or pregnancy and the dangerous episode of childbearing make it necessary for the inexperienced woman to be initiated by those who are informed in such matters. The monthly "segregation" in the closed (i.e. taboo) sacral female precinct is only a logical continuation of the initiation that has occurred in this place at the first menstruation. Childbearing occurs in this same precinct, which is the natural, social and psychological center of the female group, ruled over by the old, experienced woman . . . It is important for the basic understanding of the magical efficacy of woman and of woman as a mana figure to bear in mind that woman necessarily experienced herself as subject and object of mysterious processes and as a vessel of transformation.[49]

Can we see such possibilities today? Can we use our menstrual period, and even a return to the original biblical idea of separation—albeit now voluntary and with feminist goals—as a time to restore and rededicate ourselves as women apart from men? We live surrounded by men and patriarchy still. Could we use a monthly withdrawal from that arena into a solely female space?

Tamar Frankiel speaks of the need to escape from the societal pressure to perform equally well every day of the month, regardless of our own inner rhythms during ovulation and menstruation. "We might be forgiven for some oversights during 'that time of the month' but these are considered weaknesses rather than signs we might do better directing our energy in another path . . . we have no positive vision of this time." She goes on to suggest, "This is our solitude, our darkness, our hiddenness—an opportunity to go inward, that can lead to a spiritual focus."[50]

All of these concepts, it can be argued, lie within the traditional world view of the Torah. All of these scenarios create a beautiful aura around seclusion, but one that may be accused of apologetics. We are left to wonder who created this seclusion in ancient times: nurturing, wise women or squeamish men?

The Orthodox practice today of the period of *niddah* lasting fourteen days (that is, the addition of seven extra days, causing normal menstrual impurity to last a total of fourteen days) is a later rabbinic addendum. These additional days are sometimes called "white days" for the white cloth that must be inserted vaginally to determine that no stain of blood is left. This dictum is not found in the Torah at all.

The original biblical system of impurity was directed at keeping *all* those with discharges, both men and women, from approaching the holy district of the Temple, considered the place of God's presence. But the destruction of the Temple in 70 C.E. caused a radical shift in Jewish life which included a change of the focus of these purity laws. Without the Temple, without a center that could contract impurity, it made sense for most of the purity laws to fall into disuse. The rabbis legislated that, after the destruction of the Temple, the laws of purity for men were eliminated, but remained intact for women. Thus, while there was parallelism in the Torah for men and women's purity after emissions, the Rabbis removed that parallelism, making the purity laws relevant in the main only to women. Additionally, they claimed that, since the Temple was gone, the laws of who might approach the Tabernacle were rendered irrelevant. But women did not approach the Tabernacle directly, so the laws of ritually impurity still applied to them.

By the time of the rabbis, the focus of those laws had also shifted. Once about holiness and approach, life mixing with death, power and danger, they now became about sexual relations with a husband. Rachel Biale notes, "The justification for these laws was shifted from the realm of purity laws to the arena of sexual taboos . . . The transformation also meant a shift from the sphere of public, cultic life to the sphere of family life."[51] As Jewish society in the third century C.E. moved closer to the Roman ideal, women's role, like that of their Roman counterparts, became more and more circumscribed. The home replaced the Temple, now gone, as the center of Jewish life. The husband replaced the priest as symbol of religious authority in the home.

The notion that menstruation was a powerful symbol of life and death became painted over with ideas of female filth, pollution, and disgust at the whole female bodily experience. No longer were women secluded, either by their own design or by others' will, because they were dangerously close to the source of death and life. Today, women separate during their menses because they are forbidden to their husbands. We have lost the element of holiness, retaining only the element of taboo. Blu Greenberg puts it well, when she says, "It falls to this generation of women, Jewish women with a new sense of self, to restore that element of holiness to our bodies, our selves."[52]

Menstruation defies the borders of life and death prevalent in the Torah. The prohibitions against mixing the milk of the mother (life) with the slaughtered kid (death); against taking the mother bird with her young; and against slaughtering an animal with its young on the same day all point to the intense delineation of boundaries between living and dying, and their significance in a society that did not tolerate the mixing of opposites. Menstruation defies those boundaries, month after month. Women bleed from their life-giving organs, they give birth on the cusp of death, and yet they live. Menstruation defies male definitions of the absolute black-and-white lines of life *or* death.

> Rejoice, Fair Zion! Raise a shout, Fair Jerusalem . . . You, for your part, have released your prisoners from the dry pit, for the sake of the blood of your covenant. (Zechariah 9: 9 and 11)

It is common in the Hebrew Bible that Zion and Jerusalem are imaged as feminine. However, this is the only place in the entire Hebrew Bible where the phrase "blood of covenant" is used in relation to those "feminine entities." It is especially noteworthy that the noun, "your covenant" in the Hebrew appears in a feminine form. The traditional commentators, Rashi and Ibn Ezra among others, explain away this anomaly. They claim the feminine grammar is no indication of anything feminine, a mistake as it were. (They do not, however, make a similar claim in regards to masculine grammar used throughout the Bible, as being no indication of anything masculine!) They assert that the verse refers to the blood of circumcision.

But let us look at it in its feminine literality. It does not say "*the* covenant of blood," but rather, "*your* covenant of blood," suggesting that all "daughters of Zion" have that covenant of blood. For its sake, prisoners are released from the dry pit (death). It is through menstruation—from "adulthood" when we truly accept our responsibilities as Jews, through the elder years when bleeding stops and wisdom starts—that the entire world is saved from death. Saved from the dry pit—the pit in which there is no water—no womb, no regeneration, no rebirth.

Menstrual blood is women's covenantal blood, just as *brit milah*, circumcision, is men's. Women indeed have a *brit* inscribed in their flesh as an everlasting covenant. Women's covenant of blood is not just once, at eight days, but every month. We are "initiated" when we begin to bleed. If blood seals covenant, then women's blood seals our covenant, at puberty and through a natural flow rather than a human cut. This is a universal covenant, which all women, not just Jews, experience.

We need to rethink the Jewish quality we can ascribe to this *brit* of blood. What if girl children were named at eight days or at birth, but "brought into the covenant" at menstruation with a Jewish rite? Since at the *brit milah* one of the prayers assures us that "in your blood, you will live," for women, the blessing is perhaps even more true. The whole world, all of life in essence, lives through our blood.

Blood and water, the stuff of life. God could have had it any other way. We humans could have reproduced by fission, by splitting of atoms, by hatching from eggs, by cell mitosis. We don't. We reproduce through blood and water. We should say a blessing to announce our blood's arrival. We should bid it farewell at the end of the flow. It is our electrical charge; the holy spark that society belittles, that commerce exploits through unnecessary product lines, that patriarchal interpretation has reduced to little more than an embarrassing and dirty physical blemish. By reinterpreting it for ourselves, no matter how far-fetched that interpretation might seem, we restore ourselves to wholeness and insist on female physical holiness being part of that wholeness.

Blood and Men: A Feminist Look at Brit Milah

> God further said to Abraham, "As for you, you and your offspring to come throughout the ages shall keep my covenant. Such shall be the covenant between Me and you and your offspring to follow which you shall keep: every male among you shall be circumcised . . . Thus shall My covenant be marked in your flesh as an everlasting pact. And if any male shall fail to circumcise the flesh of his foreskin, that person shall be cut off from his kin; he has broken My covenant." (Genesis 17: 9–10, 13–14)

Perhaps no commandment in the Torah is more difficult, more divisive, more perplexing and more exclusive to men than circumcision. Is it possible for feminism to inject into this male covenantal ceremony some sense of meaning for women? Only if we allow ourselves the power of modern midrash, and expand our understanding of symbolism and metaphor in the ceremony.

Scholars believe that circumcision is one of the most ancient tribal practices ever recorded. We know that the Egyptians, Ammonites, Edomites, Moabites all practiced it. Among most cultures, circumcision took place at puberty or at marriage as a form of sacrifice, to insure fertility. The Talmud calls both a groom and a baby ready for the circumcision by the same word, *chatan*.[53] As we saw in Part I, the ancient link between removing the foreskin and marriage is further established in the biblical account of Tzipporah and Moses. In Exodus 4: 25, after circumcising their son to ward off supernatural danger, Tzipporah flings the foreskin and cries, "You are a bridegroom of blood—*chatan damim*—to me."

What is significant in the Hebrew manifestation of this ancient rite is the move from adult circumcision (Abraham) to infant circumcision (Isaac), so that the connotations of sexuality and fertility are now transported into a spiritual realm. What once was a tribal rite to ensure fruitfulness now becomes a Divine command, incumbent even upon those who may not live past childhood into marriage, even upon those who may prove to be infertile. The foreskin is considered fruitless and non-useful. Like the "uncircumcised" fruit of certain trees which cannot be eaten for the first three years (called *orlah*, the same word for foreskin), the foreskin is unripe.

The biblical focus of *brit milah*, the covenant of circumcision, is the removal of that foreskin and the subsequent releasing of blood. Since, in general, blood atones, we may assume the blood of the *brit milah* also atones. It is an offering. Perhaps this is the meaning of the verse in Genesis 9: 5, "But for your own lifeblood will I require a reckoning." We know blood belongs to God alone, as does the firstborn of human, beast and fruit. The blood of the *brit milah* is in exchange for the child's very life. The Torah teaches that an animal cannot be sacrificed before the eighth day after its birth, so male Israelites must be circumcised precisely on the eighth day, when their blood will be reckoned as a sacrifice.

Brit milah is often pictured as atonement for the general state of humanity. Aryeh Kaplan writes,

> The covenant of circumcision was one of the things that elevated Abraham and his children from the fallen state resulting from the expulsion from Eden. As a result of this covenant, the sexual act of the Jew enters the realm of the holy, and partakes of man's optimum state before his expulsion.[54]

Some have suggested *brit milah* atones for being born through female blood. For seven days a mother is made ritually "unclean" by the blood discharge, and on the eighth day she brings this baby to be circumcised—a vicarious blood offering, a sacrifice to save her from death. Circumcision then makes this baby clean, and her as well. His blood of life saves him from his mother's blood of death. Howard Eilberg-Schwartz has noted,

> Circumcision coincides with the end of a boy's impurity caused by the mother's blood at birth. The entrance of a male into the covenant thus occurs with his transition from female blood to male blood. The contrast between circumcision and the blood of birthing not only reflects differences between genders but it interprets them. Women's blood is contaminating; men's blood has the power to create covenant.[55]

The Torah requires no parallel sacrifice to cleanse a baby girl from her mother's female blood.

Sacrifices and their attendant blood must be given in only specified places, at specified times, and eaten by specified people (Leviticus 10: 16–18 and 17: 1–9). The same is true of the *brit milah*: it must be done on the eighth day, the foreskin must be removed; the one who ignores this command is, ironically, "cut off" from his people. (The same root in Hebrew, *k-r-t* is used for cutting a covenant or for cutting off as in excommunication.)

Circumcision, like sacrifice, is not only the sealing of covenant and atonement, it is also a symbol of control. To cut, whether the sexual organ or the animal's throat, is to be in command and to limit. The blood of circumcision limits; it sets bounds on who is a "member of the tribe," while setting real, physical limits on that member's sexual organ.

> And God said to Abraham, "As for your wife Sarai, you shall not call her Sarai, but her name shall be called Sarah. I will bless her, indeed I will give you a son by her. I will bless her so that she shall give rise to nations; rulers of peoples shall issue from her." (Genesis 17: 9–11)

Sarah is commanded neither to circumcise nor to be circumcised. If the cutting of the genitals was meant to ensure fertility, then surely women, for whom fertility is the guarantor of status, should have to undergo some similar rite of passage. The Torah, in limiting circumcision to men, may be purposely demeaning the cultural link of circumcision with fertility.

And if this mark signified restrained or limited sexuality, then it is even more striking that the ultimate assurance of female sexual restraint—clitoridectomy—is neither commanded, nor sanctioned, nor even mentioned. Sarah shares in the blessing, but does not have to physically sacrifice for it. As Abraham's circumcision signals new fertility, Sarah's name change signals the end of her barrenness. As he will be the progenitor of multitudes, so too will she.

The change from Sarai to Sarah entails dropping one letter, the *yud*, and replacing it with another, the *hey*. This change was not seen as arbitrary by the commentators. The Hebrew letter *hey* with the accent of "*ah*" underneath is a symbol of the feminine ending, as in, for example, *yaldah* (girl) or *na'arah* (young woman). On this name change, the seventeenth-century Polish commentator Kli Yakar suggests, "Before this episode Sarai was barren, not able to give birth, like a man. The masculine *yud* was exchanged for the feminine *hey*." Here the Torah hints of a *brit*, the notion of being covenanted, through the womb.

In Genesis 17: 15–21, God reiterates just how crucial it is that the Jewish covenant be founded through the offspring of Sarah. "My covenant I will establish through Isaac, whom Sarah will bear." This is directly juxtaposed with Abraham's circumcision, a few verses before. *Brit milah* serves as one-half of the covenantal picture; lineage through Sarah is the other.

Gary Shapiro notes that, in a metaphoric or spiritual sense, women are already circumcised, through our blood, and through our womb. On a physical level, our genitals are already open, exposed and uncovered, as the penis is after the foreskin is removed.[56] Thus circumcision actually makes men more like women. Male circumcision removes the foreskin and "opens up" or reveals the genital.

We can also see *brit milah* as a male birthing experience. Women already know the incredible bonding that occurs through the act of giving birth. From our own body comes forth new life, born in water and blood, a primordial encounter with creation itself. No matter how sensitive, how involved, how sympathetic, a man can never physically participate in that mystical encounter. Or can he? Myriel Crowley Eykamp, in an article entitled "Born and Born Again: Ritual Rebirth by Males," suggests that nearly every religious culture in the world has some sort of initiation ceremony in which there is ". . . a reappropriation or taking-over of the birthing act by the male priest . . . One must not only be born again, but born again of the male."[57]

Ritual rebirth by males is almost a universal religious

phenomenon. On one level, that means only that religious misogyny is universal. But on another level, it offers proof of men's deep longing to be able to give birth themselves. Some religions may do this through water. Judaism does it through blood, like the blood of the actual birth.

While that reappropriation can be seen as threatening to women, we can also reexamine it from a spiritual viewpoint. To be "born again of the male" is to allow the father to re-create the mystical bond in Genesis that is truly partnership with God. There ought to be a moment when the birthing experience is shared, when men birth through blood, when they connect as physically as women do. If a father "gives birth" at least symbolically to his child, he takes equal responsibility as a giver of life. Clearly, we need a rebirthing moment for the father of girl children as well.

In her book *Purity and Danger*, Mary Douglas comments on Bettelheim's view that

> psychoanalysts have overemphasized girls' envy of the male sex and overlooked the importance of boys' envy of the female sex . . . rituals which are explicitly designed to produce genital bleeding in males are intended to express male envy of female reproductive processes . . . This is merely a description of a public act. On a deeper level, what is being carved in the flesh is an image of society.[58]

In *brit milah* there is the carving of an image of what being Jewish means, into the male flesh and the male mind. We must design that image into one of a righteous, caring and fruitful society.

Circumcision is purposely imposed upon the organ that gave the baby life, which may one day perpetuate more life. It is a cut upon the sexual organ and not the earlobe or finger, as a symbol of cut, curtailed, disciplined sexuality. This interpretation is not wholly new. As early as the twelfth century, Maimonides saw the rite as reducing sexuality to a manageable level.[59] Today we need this idea rearticulated. Jewish views of sexuality include the notion that sexual pleasure is mutual, that force is violence and not love, and that human sexual encounters must be based on sanctity and not on strength.

Circumcision functions not only as ritual initiation but also as the communal ritual setting of boundaries to male sexuality. At the *brit milah* male blood is the metaphor for discipline and control over the ultimate male lack of control: unbound and dangerous sexuality. Rabbi Zalman Schachter-Shalomi writes,

> something destructive and "macho" gets refined by a bris, directing a man away from pure instinct and toward prudent judgment . . . Maybe Freud was right about the dominating power of the libido: if so, it makes sense to take that absolute power away from the penis . . . So much of what happens in sex is covenantal. Perhaps this is why Covenant has to be imposed on this organ from the very start.[60]

We cut the organ that can symbolize love or terror, endearment or violence. Here is a ceremony in which we metaphorically pronounce the limits of the male organ to all gathered. We say to this child, "We who are gathered here charge you: as your father used his organ in love to produce you, so you, too, are expected to sanctify yourself, to restrain the power of your maleness." Our community, at least in theory, rejects an unbridled masculinity. We publicly acknowledge that male sexuality is moved from the realm of the casual, hurtful, or noncommittal to the sphere of the holy, the whole, the good.

Do women need a *brit* of blood cut into their flesh to move them to the same awareness? In our society, male violence is still the norm, based on phallic authority and the fear that phallus can instill. Since we have seen how blood offers expiation throughout the Torah, can those few drops of covenantal blood be seen as atonement for male control? As cleansing of violence in a patriarchal world? Let men teach men, father to son, of vulnerability. Let our boys be entered into a circumscribed world of men whose spiritual sensitivities are increased as their phallic-centered power is decreased.

I speak from personal experience. I have three sons who were physically one with me. I held their lives inside me for nine months, nurtured and fed them through my own veins and arteries. I had to let go and allow my sons to enter the world of men, but that world often frightens and confuses me.

I wanted their *brit milah* ceremony to reflect a new understanding of disciplined masculinity, and I shared these ideas with those present. I watched how guests offered the babies blessings of wholeness, nurturing and respect for women. The Jewish world has the potential to be a safe world for me and for them, if it becomes a world of male sexuality defined by holiness, commitment and responsibility. Each of my sons' ceremonies included an acknowledgement of this new symbolism. Each baby was blessed by all the women present, holding my tallit high over him.

The common notion in our sexist world is that men are created "whole" and perfect. Circumcision negates that aggrandizement. In "sacrificing" a piece of the penis, in uncovering and revealing themselves in their most vulnerable part, in making themselves more like women, men can be made more whole.

Yet, with all this, it would be interesting to speculate on how women might have expressed covenantal relationship in the days of the Torah, had they been consulted. From the most traditional *midrashim* to the most radically new idea, these notions remain "revisions." The ceremony is still one of male bonding through some form of violence. Tender male children are taken from the safety of their mothers, the female world they have known for eight days, and given into the hands of men, who then cut them.

While the mostly male medical establishment still debates the physical usefulness of circumcision, the Jewish people hold to its spiritual usefulness. Feminists have yet to enter that discussion in full power, and on those occasions when they do, they are often accused of being traitors for merely questioning the centrality of circumcision. But it is no accident that male lawgivers chose these very ceremonies and these very symbols of control over sexuality. We need feminist *midrashim*, and serious feminist discussion, to lift both the ceremony and the participants above the masculinist suppositions, male exclusivity, and simple pain, that it contains.

Women and Water in the Torah

The first chapter of Genesis describes the earth as void and unformed, a kind of nothingness existing before creation. Yet God's spirit (*ruach* in Hebrew, which is in the feminine form) "hovers over the waters." How did the water get there? God never actually creates it. it just *is*. It always was. The primordial state of the universe is one of the dark, wet womb; the Genesis picture is a floating fetus-world. Water appears as the mother of the world.

Water gave us life in the beginning. But like blood, water can also yield death. It symbolizes both creation and destruction. In the story of Noah and the flood (Genesis 6) water brings destruction—the opposite of, the undoing of, the deconstruction of creation. Here water is not the floating stillness of birth. It is angry, stormy, tumultuous. It drowns any hope of fertility and threatens all earlier creation.

In Genesis 21, water again gives life. After Hagar and Ishmael are cast out of Abraham's house into the desert, they nearly die. Hagar looks up and sees a well, and gives her thirsty son drink before it is too late. Here, water revives and restores.

Our matriarch Rebecca proves her mettle at a well, where she gives water to Abraham's servant and to his animals as well, demonstrating her kindness and compassion, together with her suitability as a wife for Isaac. Their son Jacob meets our matriarch Rachel at a well, and there, in an act of chivalry, he unrolls a stone that has blocked the water source.

As a leitmotif, water dominates the story of the Exodus. Moses is placed in it and later saved from it. His name means "drawn out of the water." The waters of the Nile turn to blood and then to water again; the Israelites walk through the sea on dry land. For the Israelites water is life; for the Egyptians who are drowned in it, death. At the shores of the sea Moses and Miriam each sing a song of praise to God's wondrous redemption. Miriam's name itself contains a reference to water: *yam*, the sea.

Moses meets his wife, Tzipporah, by a well. The people, in all their wanderings, grumble for water. From water, the original birth fluids of the creation of the world, the Israelite nation is born. It is Moses' salvation at his birth; but it is his downfall when he strikes the rock hoping to get it to spring forth water, instead of speaking to the rock as God commanded. When Moses dies at the ripe old age of one hundred and twenty, the Torah remembers his relationship to water and records that his "moisture"—a euphemism for sexual potency—had not abated.

We have seen how powerful the symbol of blood is in the Torah. Blood comes only from inside the body; it is produced there and has no outside source of its own. In modern times, if we need more, we must get it from another body. Water is blood's symbolic partner, but also its symbolic opposite.

Though the human body is composed of water, if we need more, we can go almost anywhere to find it. We cannot produce the water we need to live. We find its sources and there it is for us, drinkable, bathable, giving life to the faint and sick. It births us. It sustains us. But it is not truly *of us*. Lakes, rivers and streams attest to creative powers outside of the human realm. Rain falls without our exertion, independent of our will. No wonder our ancestors, in their desert environment, chose water as the ultimate symbol of purity and purification. It transforms us because it is both in us and independent of us. The leper, the *niddah*, the new initiate, all bathe in it to experience a change in status and a form of rebirth.

Water has an organic connection to women as the fluid of birth, for a baby floats in a sac of water inside its mother. Water also acquires a connection to women in the Torah as each matriarch meets her husband at the well, and as Miriam's life stories all take place around water. Thus the *mikveh*, the traditional pool or collection of living water used for immersions, has become a symbol of rebirth for Jewish women.

Elyse Goldstein

A Feminist Reexamination of Mikveh

Among the traces of living substances
The marine colors of colorless form
Ever so slowly submerged
In timeless, spaceless, motionless mode
In the water, life-giving, life-sustaining
As the foetus' domain.
Sarah-Louise Giroux 3 Elul 5754
(Written upon her conversion to Judaism at the mikveh*)*

Can we take this traditional water ritual and give it a new twist? Perhaps feminists can reappropriate this ancient ritual and see water as a powerfully positive reaffirmation of our wholeness and our purity.

Physically, the *mikveh* is a small pool of "living water" about the size of a jacuzzi, but without jets. The water must be part rain water, or water taken from a natural source, so that it is truly "living." Traditionally, those ready to change their existential status go to *mikveh* to mark that shift. You go into the water as one kind of person, you come out another. People converting to Judaism are initiated in the *mikveh*. Brides about to become married women go, before the wedding ceremony. Some grooms now choose to go as well.

In the Orthodox community, the most common use of the *mikveh* is by married women after their menstrual cycle. During those seven days, and for an additional seven afterward, menstruating wives have sexually separated from their husbands, as legislated by the Torah in the laws of *niddah* in Leviticus. It has become inexorably linked to having a husband, to making oneself ready to return to sexual relations with one's male partner, and to being connected to a man. According to tradition (although some argue that this is not law), divorced or single women, and lesbians, even though menstruating, do not go to *mikveh*. It is assumed they are not having sexual relations with a man, perpetuating the connection of *mikveh* with women in relationship to men.

No matter how we try to skirt the issue, no matter how we rewrite history or remake images, the bottom line is that a traditional rationale sees the *mikveh* as the last necessary step before resuming sexual relations within a heterosexual marriage, a step commanded by God. Any other reason for going—to spiritually renew oneself after one's cycle, to cleanse from the menstrual "whisper of death," to link oneself to Jewish women's "herstory," to reground after feeling cramps and bloating, to deal with a trauma like divorce or chemotherapy—are deemed "interesting" and "unique" and perhaps even "lovely." But according to strict traditionalists, these reasons are secondary and superfluous. This adds up to a great deal of resentment toward the *mikveh* among liberal and non-Orthodox women. We need to redefine the use of the *mikveh* as an act of "taking back the water."

I am a Reform Jew, a rabbi and a feminist, and I go to the *mikveh* every month. For me, it is an experience of reappropriation, a rebirth: first of myself as a woman and a Jew, a regrounding after my period or after times of stress or upheaval; then a rebirth of the entire *mikveh* ritual itself. The *mikveh* has been taken from me by sexist interpretations, by my experiences with Orthodox "family purity" committees who run communal *mikvaot* as Orthodox monopolies, by a history of male biases, fears of menstruation and superstitions. I return each month to "take back the water."[61]

To take back the water means we reject its principal import as a tool of marriage and we open up other avenues for meaning. To take back the water means to open the *mikveh* up to women not attached to men. In order to do that, we may have to build alternative *mikvaot*, run by women, for women, following women's rules, not funded or run "behind the scenes" by male rabbis with family purity laws or their own denominational territories to protect.

For those in small towns, using a lake or stream, or a dip in the ocean, is a wonderful alternative. Go in groups at times when privacy is assured. Where there is a community Jewish center, steps could be taken to ensure a truly cross-denominational representation building a small *mikveh* on a site which already has a swimming pool. Women who have jacuzzis in their homes might agree to turn the hot tub into a *mikveh* once a month!

To take back the waters means to dip on Rosh Chodesh, when the moon and the sea and women's cycles become one. To take back the water means to open the *mikveh* during the day, so women don't have to sneak in under cover of darkness. (If we aren't ashamed of our bodies, why do we need to hide our immersions? If we reject the notion that *mikveh* is only for the right to resume sex with our husbands, we won't have to be modest about going.)

As Miriam's well gave strength to the Israelites, so too can the *mikveh* give strength back to Jewish women. Water is the symbol of birth—now it can be a symbol of conscious feminist rebirth. To take back the water means to separate it from the laws of *niddah*, so that women feel free to experience its spiritual power even if they do not feel moved to acknowledge their own menstruation, menopause, or sexual separation from their partners. To take back the water means to turn the *mikveh* into a Jewish women's center: with Torah learning and books available, maybe even feminist classes, not just wig advertisements and pamphlets on keeping a kosher home.

We can appropriate the "spiritual cleansing" properties of immersion, called in Hebrew *tevilah*, for a variety of other occasions. In the past ten years, I have witnessed the powerful emotional response of converts and I have sought to re-create that experience for Jews in other life situations.

I myself have experienced this transformative power. The first time I went to *mikveh* was before my ordination. I wanted to be "clean" as I approached the day I began my spiritual calling. I knew that ordination day itself would be moving, but also hectic and public. I wanted a private way to prepare. Because I was not married at the time, the woman in charge of overseeing immersions, sometimes called the "*mikveh* lady," was hesitant and unsure. She needed a category into which I could fit. Somehow I managed to convince her that I was like a bride! I felt the *mikveh* experience in a deeply personal way as I cleansed myself of personal doubts and obstacles to my ordination.

I used *mikveh* again after I completed the thirty-day mourning period, *sheloshim*, for my sister. The intensity of that month and my own grief was so strong that I needed an equally strong ritual to mark my reentry into normal life. The *mikveh* soothed me, and reassured me that life could somehow go on.

I call the use of the *mikveh* for people who have experienced radical, intense life changes or trauma, "spiritual therapy." I use the *mikveh* as a tool for that kind of pastoral encounter. I remember the first situation that arose enabling me to offer the *mikveh* in this way. A woman who had been a congregant of mine sought a spiritual outlet after she had been raped by the handyman she had hired to work in her home. She was a single mother and emotionally fragile. After months of therapy, she still seemed to be stuck on her feelings of being "dirty." Her therapist, knowing how involved she was in her Judaism and how much comfort that brought her, came to me to inquire whether there was some Jewish ritual that could help this woman remove the feeling of being "tainted." I suggested the *mikveh* could be a tool for cleansing both her body and soul.

We tried it. In the water she meditated on a clean, pure image of herself, shining and shimmering with light. The *mikveh* performed no magic and she, of course, stayed in therapy. However, her therapist reported that having a Jewish framework in which this woman could rid herself of the "stain" she felt, was crucial to the successful completion of therapy and her ability to go back to work, synagogue, friends and family with a sense of peace.

Since that incident, in every therapeutic situation when I have suggested the use of *mikveh*, the response has been overwhelmingly positive. Some Jewish therapists and pastoral counsellors now see the link between sexuality, spirituality and spiritual purity and are either using the *mikveh* as a tool with clients, or referring them to rabbis who will take them. Situations in which rabbis might suggest *mikveh* have been rape, incest, marital infidelity and reconciliation, infertility, loss of pregnancy, menopause, invasive surgery, milestone birthdays, end of mourning, crisis points and life-changing situations.

Of course, *mikveh* does not take the place of therapy. It is not voodoo. It will not bring fertility or good luck and it cannot radically change personalities or situations. It will never cure deep-rooted problems. It offers no quick-fix, but acts as one part of a healing process which expressed in a Jewish context. In fact, it is probably more symbolism than anything else: a bath unlike any other bath. According to therapist Yonah Klem,

> at home, the bathroom is familiar and the water, the same that usually comes out of the tap. Leaving the ease and familiarity of home to bathe in a different bathroom, and then to go further to immerse in the natural waters in a pool that has no counterpart anywhere else, also builds expectation and intent.[62]

Like any new ritual, the use of the *mikveh* as a spiritual tool requires preparation and creativity. It also requires new liturgy to accompany the ceremony and an open, supportive atmosphere. We generally do a good job of marking life's traumas and transforming moments with gatherings and parties. The *mikveh* helps us frame those life-changing occurrences as moments in Jewish time. Because there is little precedent for such nontraditional *mikveh* ceremonies, we have the freedom and flexibility to create rituals that speak to the heart and move people to positive action. We can use the *mikveh* in as many new ways as we want, inventing as we go along. Some ceremonies will be written by rabbis and some by the participants themselves. Some will have music and others will use candles. I have encouraged mothers of the bride to offer blessings as she dips in the water. One man converting to Judaism sang a song he had written as he entered the water.[63]

Rachel Adler has written,

> When Jewish women who were not Orthodox appropriated my reframing of immersion in the *mikveh* to mark occurrences for which no ritual had existed, they taught me an important lesson about the possibility of salvage . . . The makers have imbued these rituals with a different understanding of what purity means.[64]

The *mikveh* is now about salvage: salvage of a woman's reality, salvage of ourselves as spiritually whole but spiritually fragile, salvage of a tradition that was once put upon us but which we have embraced as our own. Salvage is a way of feminists embracing a tradition with a potential that exists beyond that particular tradition's narrow scope.

Some ask: Why bother at all to take back the water? Why not simply abandon an institution which makes us so uncomfortable? My answer: Because we have so little that is ours. We put on a *tallis*, but in doing so we share a man's ritual garb. We need symbols we can own, not merely rent. The water belongs to us: It is the fluid of our own bodies and a deeply moving experience of connection to Mother Earth. We acknowledge that to be female is to bleed. To bleed is to give and also lose life. To give and also lose life is to be dangerously close to the edge. To be close to the edge requires regrounding, re-centering, a rebirth. To be reborn is to enter the waters of the womb once again. To do that, women must be in control of the process *and* the product, of the intention and the action. We are now in the process of, as Adler calls it, salvage.

I believe we can also reappropriate the traditional use of *mikveh*. If menstruation as the symbol of power and danger can be reappropriated to the feminist agenda, its symbolism can be celebrated with the use of *mikveh*. The goal is to have a positive physicality, a cycle that begins with blessings and ends with blessings, the first and last time, and every time. Water and blood, blood and water—the stuff we are made of, we stand in awe of. We acknowledge our own power and our own limitations.

If the goal is to also to acknowledge our sensuality, what could be more luxurious than this long bath in nature's mother-waters?

The water softly caresses us as we immerse naked and let it lap and lick and touch every part of our sexual being. We dip with our fingers and toes spread; but with our legs spread too, so the water touches the vagina, and we feel its coolness on the core of our sexual heat. Then we pray for sexual satisfaction this month, for joining, for union; we pray for playfulness and abandon. The waters rebirth us as sexual beings as much as Jewish beings.

This "water of Eden" carries us back to our first encounter with Lilith, that sexual, sensual mate of Adam, that free part of ourselves which we now immerse.

PART III

God, Goddess, Gender and the Torah

A Meditation on the Feminine Nature of Shekhinah

Shekhinah is She Who Dwells Within,
The force that binds and patterns creation.
She is Birdwoman, Dragonlady, Queen of the Heavens,
Opener of the Way.
She is Mother of the Spiritworld, Morning and Evening
  Star,
Dawn and Dusk.
She is Mistress of the Seas, Tree of Life,
Silvery Moon, Fiery Sun.
All these are Her Names.
Shekhinah is Changing Woman, Nature herself,
Her own Law and Mystery.
She is cosmos, dark hole, fiery moment of beginning.
She is dust cloud, nebulae, the swirl of galaxies.
She is gravity, magnetic field,
the paradox of waves and particles.
Shekhinah is unseen dark, invisible web,

Creatrix of complex systems,
expanding, contracting, spiralling, meandering,
The beginning of Wisdom.
Shekhinah is Grandmother, Grandfather,
Unborn Child,
Shekhinah is life loving itself into being . . .

Rabbi Lynn Gottlieb

Introduction

In the first part of this book we met our foremothers as characters in the ongoing drama of the formation of the Jewish people. There they acted as individual women, and as archetypes of women in general. In the second part, we explored women as physical beings. We saw how the Torah views the functions of menstruation and childbearing as central to the notion of being female.

Equally crucial to being female is a sense of what I would call "the spirituality of femaleness." As feminists, we see being female as a primary aspect of our self-definition. It is a central part of our sense of who we are and how we fit into the world. Being female not only means something; it also gives our lives meaning.

Thus, in Part Three, we look at women as spiritual beings. Into that discussion comes the question of finding meaning in our femaleness in the Torah. We search, often between the lines, for vestiges of what our foremothers might have believed, or ways they might have worshipped. Did they bring to their Hebrew tents memories, or reverent but hidden ceremonies, filled with feminine imagery and iconography? Were these a legacy of an even earlier, more matriarchal than patriarchal time, still remembered?

We find references to pagan practices throughout the Torah, always vilified and rejected. Our ancestors seem terrified of what they called the "abominations" of worship traditions in the peoples around them. Yet it seems reasonable to argue that the Torah would not have had to admonish the Israelites against participating in those rites so often, had there not been a fascination and attraction to those pagan practices in the first place. Without suggesting a return to such practices in their original forms, it still behooves us to explore them for the light they may shed on women's spirituality in the biblical period. That light can be used and adapted in today's search for meaning and spirituality among modern Jewish women.

There is a growing interest among feminists in the image of the goddess. In such imagery, the biological functions of women—birth and lactation at the very least—were elevated, and we can only wonder if such positive imagery led to a respectful sense of self among women. Women of today need a meaningful religious vocabulary around our biology as well as around our concerns of fertility and fruitfulness, a vocabulary that has been paltry in traditional Judaism. Thus, we should not belittle the appeal these ancient ways had for our foremothers or might still have for us today.

New Age practices, neo-paganism, and modern goddess worship attract Jewish feminists with their creativity, their physicality and their visceral attachment to the female experience. This spirituality centers on us as women, on our biology, our intuition, and our connection with nature and the moon. Finding parallels in the Torah leads us to the very real possibility of adaptation and a Jewish context for our spiritual search. Bringing the discussion back to the source helps us find an original biblical vocabulary for our perceived needs of today.

Any serious discussions of Jewish feminist issues must eventually come to the question of language. How do we choose to express our relationship to God? As Jews, we find ourselves engaged with the God of the Torah, whether we personally believe in a supernatural Being, or in a spiritual force, or in some amorphous indefinable personal connection to the universe. We must ask if the language of our relationship has some effect on the relationship itself.

As children, we are taught, through stories, about the God of the Torah. We come to know God as a King, a Father, an all-powerful and mighty Being. But as we grow into adulthood, and we redefine our beliefs in a more sophisticated way, we often find ourselves uncomfortable with those simplistic childhood images. Our spiritual experience, and thus our spiritual vocabulary, has increased and broadened, but our prayer-language has not. We end by exploring the implications for all Jews of male imagery and male language for God.

These issues come last, though they are primary concerns. They grow out of the first two parts of this book, because once we have met our role models, and we meet our physical selves, we are ready to meet our spiritual selves.

We begin by uncovering the vestiges of female imagery and goddess symbolism in the Torah. In Part Three we explore the remnants of the female spirit in the Torah, we question assumptions of what paganism was and is, and we ask about the place of the goddess in Judaism today.

Searching for the Female Spirit in the Torah

Creation

In the beginning [when] God created the heaven and the earth—the earth being unformed [Hebrew: *tohu*] and void, with darkness over the deep [Hebrew: *tehom*] and the wind [or spirit] of God sweeping over the water—God said, "Let there be light" and there was light. (Genesis 1: 1–3)

The world is created through both words and water. God speaks and the world comes into being, while a wind from God sweeps over the water. The word for wind, *ruach*, a feminine word, is also the word for spirit. The primordial world is described as watery and unformed. Like an embryo, it floats, still without a definite shape. As an embryo's gender is unknown to the mother for at least the first three months, in a state of commingled male/female identity, so too the world is a commingling of male and female in the first primordial state.

Peter Graves and Raphael Patai have shown that the words *tohu* (the unformed) and *tehom* (the deep) may be versions of the earlier names Tehomot, or Tiamat, the Babylonian mother goddess, who menstruated for three years and three days to provide the sea of creation.[65] In the Hebrew text, these words never take the definite article, "*the* deep" or "*the* unformed," which might associate them with those earlier goddesses' names. Akkadian epics tell of waters threatening to destroy the world, and Tehom is their Queen. Our ancestors were familiar with these myths of creation by sea and sea-mother goddesses. They knew that the overriding theme of such stories was the conquering or containing of the female element—the wild and uncontrolled goddess symbolized by the chaotic waters of the sea—in order for creation to proceed.

In the Hebrew text, it is the Hebrew God, known here as Elohim or by the four-letter name YHVH, who must struggle against the sea, the water that gives birth to the world. He replaces the water as the one who gives birth to the world. Darkness, Disorder, Tiamat, who were goddesses, powers, and objects of worship for the neighbors of the ancient Hebrews, are now objects of derision, to be usurped and perfected by YHVH.

Snakes and Rods

> Now the serpent was the shrewdest of all the beasts that the Lord God had made. He said to the woman, "Did God really say, 'You shall not eat of any tree in the garden?'" . . . And the Lord God said to the woman, "What is this that you have done?" The woman replied, "The serpent tricked me, and I ate." Then the Lord God said to the snake, "Because you did this, more cursed shall you be than all the cattle and all the beasts. On your belly shall you crawl and dirt shall you eat all the days of your life. And I will put enmity between you and the woman . . ." (Genesis 3: 1 and 13–15)

Eve and the snake have a relationship, strange yet somehow close. He cons her into eating the forbidden fruit. She listens to the snake, and seems to trust him. We know of the association of snakes with oracular goddesses from Greek evidence at Delphi.[66] The name Eve, Hava in Hebrew, means "snake" in ancient Sumerian. This subtle pun was intended for the readers of the day, who were already familiar with the dual symbolism of the serpent: both male phallic power (the snake that stiffens and becomes a powerful rod in Egypt) and female sexuality (Hectate, the dark moon goddess, is partly snake in form). In myths of the surrounding peoples, it was commonly held that snakes copulate with women.[67] Adam, the woman's male partner, now takes that role. Indeed, part of the woman's punishment for taking the forbidden fruit is a new-found enmity between her and the snake. Her sexual desire shall be for her husband, rather than for the snake. And *he* will rule over her, instead of the snake goddess ruling over her.

The snake, symbol of the female, must be overcome by the male. Adam and God together will control the serpent: Adam by ignoring its pleas to eat the fruit and God by punishing it and ending its long association with women. We see this symbolism of the male conquering the female, god conquering goddess, later in Moses' use of the snake/rod. The Egyptians worshipped the snake goddesses, named Meretseger and Renenutet. When Moses throws down the rod and it becomes a snake and then a rod again, he subdues *their* symbol, the serpent. He claims the power of the Hebrew God over the Egyptian goddesses; the power of the erect phallus (the rod) over the pliable female (the slithering snake). His rod consumes theirs.

The Hebrew name Hava is directly explicated in the Genesis text as meaning "mother of all living," which seems more of a title than a name, akin to "earth mother." The name Hava may also be a Hebraicized version of the goddess Heba, wife of the Hittite storm god, whose worship in Jerusalem is evidenced in letters from the Jebusite King Abdu-Heba (slave of the goddess Heba) to Pharaoh Amenhotep III in the fourteenth century B.C.E.[68] The Torah's Eve becomes the mother goddess sublimated, co-opted and no longer worshipped. She is humanized, dethroned and disguised, though perhaps not completely to our ancestors, since today we are no longer familiar with the historical roots of her name and her function.

Matriarchy/Patriarchy and Lineage

Because birth was so obviously from the mother, the concepts of paternity and fatherhood were not clearly delineated in earlier times. Therefore it would be natural for children to take the name of their mother's clan or tribe. However, once the Torah established biological paternity as essential, absolute marital fidelity was required from women, so as to ensure knowledge of the father's identity. Inheritance and lines of descent, the "begots" of the Torah, now went through the father rather than the mother. This has important consequences in the laws of inheritance. Cyrus Gordon noted that ancient Egypt subscribed to the idea of matrilineal inheritance, where possessions and estates passed through the mother.[69] The freed Israelites, intent on establishing a social order very different and in marked contrast to that of Egypt, enforced patrilineal inheritance as a mark and seal of that difference.

This may be one of the critical reasons feminists are so interested in pre-biblical religion. Theology and sociology go together; that is, the subordination of Israelite women is connected to the emergence in Torah of a preoccupation with clan, patrilineal descent, and worship of one unseen, unnamed yet male-imagined God. Loyalty to the One God is akin to loyalty to the one husband.

According to Graves and Patai, the book of Genesis emphasizes a struggle of the newly patriarchal Hebrews against their matriarchal neighbors. Vestiges of an earlier matriarchal society are apparent throughout the Torah. For example, children of the same father but different mothers are permitted to marry (as in the story of Amnon and Tamar in II Samuel 13), suggesting such half-siblings were, by their mothers, actually members of different clans, and were not considered to be marrying into the same family.

This move from matriarchy to patriarchy is seen most clearly in the story of Isaac meeting Rebecca. In Genesis 24, we see Abraham's servant sent to find a wife for Isaac from among Abraham's kinsmen, the patriarchal line. After the servant presents Rebecca with gifts and asks for lodging in her father's house, she tells all that has happened to "her mother's household," the matriarchal line. Abraham commands the servant to take a wife from his "father's house" and expects his brother's daughter to leave her home and come to live with Isaac in Isaac's patriarchal tribe. But this is not the custom in Rebecca's tribe/home, for the servant wonders, "What if the woman does not follow me?" In Rebecca's culture, the husband follows the wife into *her* tribe, and the servant is worried that Rebecca might reject this notion of "marrying out" of her own group. Rebecca's mother and brother Laban play a large and central role in the betrothal negotiations. The father is absent, either deceased or, in a matriarchal society, not essential to the marriage agreement. After taking Rebecca as a wife, Isaac consummates the marriage in his mother's tent, attesting to the marriage's acceptability to the matriarchal line.

Seeing the move from matriarchy to patriarchy may help us understand Rebecca's "ruse" in switching Esau and Jacob to secure their father's blessing and inheritance rights. Rebecca comes from a tradition of matrilineal inheritance, where she would be able to achieve the ends she desired without the use of manipulation. In that tradition, perhaps the youngest child of the mother naturally inherited. However, in her new patriarchal environment, all she can do to secure her choice is to maneuver her sons around their feeble father. Rebecca has some sense of her "old" previous power, which informed her plan and her subterfuge.

And the switch plays a part in the story of Laban. Jacob has married the two daughters of his mother's brother Laban. After working for Laban for fourteen years to marry both Leah and Rachel, Jacob decides it is time to take his wives, children and livestock, and leave to return to his father's home. He has lived all this time with his wives' family. Laban, meeting up with his fleeing nephew Jacob, says, "The daughters are *my* daughters," meaning, you lived with your wife's family, as is the custom here. Rabbi W. Gunther Plaut suggests this is an indication of Laban placing Jacob's marriages in a special Assyrian legal category called *erebu*, in which the husband lives with his wife's family and if he leaves he cannot take his wife or her belongings with him.

Plaut also suggests that another example of matriarchal marriage can be found in the early Genesis statement "Therefore a man leaves his mother and cleaves to his wife" as an echo of the custom of having a man become part of his wife's family and household.[70]

The preoccupation, in the Jacob story, with the careful reading of which mothers gave birth to which sons also points to a matriarchal focus. Graves suggests the early history of the Israelite tribes centered on matriarchal heads; that is, not on which of Jacob's sons headed the tribe but from which of four women the tribe descended: Leah, Rachel or their maidservants Zilpah and Bilhah. Thus the Torah stories of enmity between the twelve sons or of enmity between the two wives would be historical explanations retrojected back into mythological stories to explain why the tribal structure existed as it did. He proposes there was a "Leah–Rachel federation" of tribes later called "Israel." Zilpah's sons were "tributaries" of the Leah tribes, since Zilpah is described as the servant of Leah; Bilhah's sons were "tributaries" of the Rachel tribes. The pillar erected as a memorial to Rachel after her death in childbirth with Benjamin may have been a marker of a new federation between the Rachel tribes and the Leah tribes, which would now include the tribe of Benjamin. From this point of view, the rivalry between Leah and Rachel is political rather than familial.

He further suggests that there may have been a tribe of Dinah. The Dinah tradition, now lost, represents an independent tribe of the Leah federation, which had a matriarchal structure. Her rape by Shechem mythologizes her small tribe being overrun by the Amorites of Shechem. Her allies, the Leah tribes of Simeon and Levi, take revenge by massacring them, after which her identity as a tribe is lost and she is heard from no more.

Pagan Symbolism in the Rachel Story

> Jacob left Beer-Sheva and set out for Haran. He came upon a certain place and stopped there for the night, for the sun had set. Taking one of the stones of that place, he put it under his head and lay down in that place. He had a dream: a ladder was set on the ground with its top reaching the sky, and angels of God were going up and down on it . . . Early in the morning, Jacob took the stone that he had put under his head and set it up as a pillar and poured oil on the top of it. (Genesis 28: 10–12, and 18)

The word "place" appears three times in the first three sentences of this narrative. Surely Jacob has not chosen to stop and rest in any ordinary spot. After his powerful dream, Jacob chooses one of the stones and erects it, anointing it as a pillar, *matzaivah* in Hebrew. When his beloved Rachel dies, Jacob again erects a pillar.

He names the place where the dream occurred Beth El, house of God, but also "house of the god El," a well-known Canaanite shrine from before Jacob's time. Cone-shaped pillars anointed with oil, associated with worship of the moon goddess, are called *baetylos* in Greek, likely a borrowing from the Phoenician of the Hebrew word *Beth El*.

Is Jacob familiar with the history and association of pillars? The Torah later prohibits Israelites from erecting them for worship purposes (Exodus 23: 24), because pillars, again the word *matzaivah*, are used in pagan rites.

When Jacob leaves his father-in-law Laban, his wife Rachel "steals" her father's *teraphim*, or idols (Genesis 31). The text doesn't tell us whether she wishes to hurt him by stealing something he loves, or whether she loves those idols and wants them for herself, as a reminder of home and her childhood. The Torah shows its distaste for the *teraphim* by suggesting that Rachel sat on them during her menstrual period, when the Israelites claim a woman's touch defiles anything, particularly a sacred object.

Laban catches up with Jacob and his wives and demands the return of those sacred statues. He and Jacob then erect yet another pillar of stones, and there swear by their "ancestral deities" that they will not be hostile to each other. They spend the night on the heights, the same word used for the Canaanite "high places" ordered destroyed later, in Deuteronomy. In the morning Laban leaves, without his *teraphim*. Rachel has managed to bring with her, into this new patriarchal worship system, the last remnants of her former polytheism. Perhaps she intended to set up a shrine. Rachel is not condemned for her use of the *teraphim*, nor for her later use of mandrakes to promote fertility. Mandrakes were used, according to Ugaritic documents, in fertility rites.

Dinah and the Daughters of the Land

> Now Dinah, the daughter whom Leah had borne to Jacob, went out to visit the daughters of the land. Shechem son of Hamor the Hivite, chief of the country, saw her, and took her and lay with her by force . . . Jacob heard that he had defiled his daughter Dinah, but since his sons were in the field with his cattle, Jacob kept silent until they came home . . . Meanwhile, Jacob's sons, having heard the news, came in from the field. The men were very distressed and angry, because he had committed an outrage in Israel by lying with Jacob's daughter—a thing not to be done! . . . Jacob said to Simeon and Levi, "You have brought trouble to me, making me odious among the inhabitants of the land" . . . But they answered, "Should our sister be treated like a whore?" (Genesis 34: 1–2, 5, 7, 30–31)

Where was Dinah going? Who were "the daughters of the land" and why would she visit them? Shechem is in Canaan, home and center of the worship of the goddess Astarte, worship that may have included engaging in sexual initiation rites. Some goddess societies required virgins to sacrifice their virginity during their temple rites.

It is tempting to imagine Dinah's attraction to, or curiosity about, this women's custom, feelings shared by many of the Canaanite women around her. She "went out" to see what it was all about. The Torah censors the rest of the details. It is purposely vague about her destination, why she went, and what the daughters of the land were doing. Perhaps they attended a women's festival. Perhaps they visited the annual women's mourning for the dying and rising god Tammuz, about which we will learn more later. Perhaps they went to participate in the sexual rites attached to goddess-worship, or maybe they simply wanted to meet at the well and exchange stories. The suggestion that this mysterious visit to the Canaanite "orgies" caused Dinah's downfall supports the theory that it may have been common in those days for Israelite women to make such visits.

When Shechem sees her, he assumes—rightly, in his mind—that she is "available," that she is participating in these rites, as the other women of the land are doing. He assumes he can "have her." When he finds out he cannot, he becomes outraged and violent. Why would she refuse if she stands at the gate of the temple with the other women prepared to participate? Does he even know she is a Hebrew?

No wonder this event scandalized her brothers so. Not only did she attend the goddess-worship and sexual rite, but Shechem forced her to participate, which would have been, as the brothers say, "an outrage in Israel."

The brothers of Dinah deceive Shechem into thinking they will allow Dinah to be given to him as a wife, if only he and the men of his town will agree to be circumcised. They do, and while the men are in pain, Dinah's brothers massacre them all. When Jacob complains that his sons' retaliatory attack may injure his reputation and create lasting enmity, they reply, "Should our sister be treated like a whore?" There they use the common word for whore, *zonah*, to cast more serious aspersions on Shechem. They choose to use the pejorative, the epithet, rather than the word *kadesha*, which literally translates as "sacred one" but may refer to participants in the Canaanite temple's sexual initiation rites, or more simply, Canaanite priestesses. Should their sister be treated as a common whore, even when she was taking part in (or merely observing) a sacred rite?

The story has links with the later story of Tamar in Genesis 38. Disguising herself as a *kadesha*, no common whore but a participant in rites, she plants herself where a passing Israelite could participate in those rites with her. This presupposes, of course, that Israelite men were wont to do so. Judah unashamedly enjoys the services of Tamar while she is dressed as a *kadesha*. Our "pious" men of old seem to have been attracted to pagan practices, too.

Moses and the Calf

> When the people saw that Moses was so long in coming down from the mountain, the people gathered against Aaron and said to him, "Come, make us a god who shall go before us, for that man Moses, who brought us from the land of Egypt—we know not what has happened to him . . . And all the people took off the gold rings that were in their ears and brought them to Aaron. This he took from them and cast in a mold and made it into a molten calf. And they exclaimed,

> 'These are your gods, O Israel, who brought you out of the land of Egypt!'" When Aaron saw this, he built an altar before it. And Aaron announced: "Tomorrow shall be a festival of the Lord!" Early the next day, the people offered up burnt offerings and brought sacrifices of well being; they sat down to eat and drink, and then rose to play. (Exodus 32: 1–5)

What was this golden calf? The people asked Aaron to make a image of what they thought resembled the Israelite god YHVH, and therefore Aaron proclaimed the next days as a "festival to YHVH." Perhaps they needed a molten image of Moses himself, since they did not know where he was or if he would ever return; they wanted to turn Moses into a god, symbolized by a golden calf. Aaron gave in to their request rather easily. In later commentary, the rabbis suggest that Aaron was stalling for time, thinking that if he asked people for their gold, they would refuse. He was surprised that after the gold had been thrown into the fire, a molten calf came out (Exodus 32: 24).

But could it be that Aaron felt jealous of Moses and still clung to the old ways of Egypt, and, like the common people, longed for the tangible manifestations of the gods and goddesses they had known?

The golden calf was a familiar symbol from Egypt for the Israelites. One of the most sacred symbols of the Egyptians was Osiris, a bull god conceived when the moon fastened onto a cow in heat. The maternal and nurturing aspects of the moon goddess were also represented by a cow, whose horns suggested the horned moon. In her human form the goddess was often depicted in the company of a goat, a calf or a bull.

The last line of the passage shows the nature of those old ways; they "rose up *l'tzahek*." The Hebrew word *l'tzahek*, translated here as "play," has a sexual connotation. The same word is used, for example, when Isaac and Rebecca are in Gerar (Genesis 26), and when Isaac embraces or fondles Rebecca. The word appears again in the Joseph story, when Joseph is accused by Potiphar's wife of trying to seduce her.

Female Imagery and Paganism

> You must not make a covenant with the inhabitants of the land, for they will whore after their gods and sacrifice to their gods and invite you, and you will eat of their sacrifices. And when you take wives from among their daughters for your sons, their daughters will whore after their gods and will cause your sons to lust after their gods. (Exodus 34: 14–16)

Within the context of the Torah's unrelenting fear of idolatry lies the association of women with that idolatry. In biblical metaphor, God and the people of Israel are in a covenantal relationship like a marriage, which must be monogamous. Israel plays either the loyal wife or the wanton woman. When Israel goes astray after other gods, she is "whoring." The word "whore" is not merely metaphor; it appears as an assessment of the religious traditions surrounding the Israelites. They saw the sexual activities of goddess-worshippers and felt a need to separate themselves in the most obvious way possible from sexual activity connected to that worship.

Foreign wives were often suspected of loyalty to the old ways. They brought not only their idols, but their love for and fond memories of their worship of those idols. Coming from matriarchal traditions, tracing their ancestry through the maternal lineage, such women might well find it difficult to give up their household religion. Israel is constantly chastised for "whoring" after Moabite women or after "alien gods."

Many of the Torah's associations of paganism are in reference to matriarchy, powerful women's traditions, and foreign women. In seeing the move in the Torah from matriarchy to patriarchy, we also see the Torah's shift away from the accompanying symbols and systems of matriarchy, which included worship of a goddess. Thus the rejection of goddess-worship is linked to a rejection of matriarchy, and the rejection of matriarchy is linked to rejection of the worship of a goddess.

It is nearly impossible to speak about paganism or goddess worship and the Torah without being branded a traitor to monotheism. Paganism is considered bad, orgiastic and primitive. The female spirit in the Torah, whenever it is expressed through pagan or goddess-centered symbolism, has been either staunchly renounced or supplanted by some other "higher" form of theology.

In their experimentation with female terms for God, feminists have been branded as pagan. While indeed some invoke the names of the ancient goddesses, others turn to traditional expressions of God's inherent femininity, such as the Kabbalistic "Shekhinah," or names for God with mothering motifs from the Tanach itself (which will be discussed at the end of this section). Critics of these ways of looking at God invoke cries of child sacrifice and orgiastic sexuality. But in light of the challenge offered by religious and political feminism to the dominant male culture, we should ask whether this deeply ingrained Jewish rejection of goddess images is a rejection of true paganism, a rejection of how we imagine paganism was practiced, or simply a rejection of any feminine imagery of God at all. When the fear of the repercussions of female imagery—female inclusion and female leadership, for example—is cloaked in the charge of paganism, and we accept that paganism by definition must be bad, the feminist attempt at including female language in our communal life is successfully thwarted, and the voices of those calling for change are silenced. The use of the word "pagan" successfully stops all dialogue. Why are we so afraid?

Paganism, it is argued, sullies the preferred monotheism. Cynthia Ozick writes,

> . . . [for] "King of the Universe" we are advised to substitute the term "Queen of the Universe." The answer stuns with its crudity . . . Millennia after the cleansing purity of Abraham's vision of the One Creator, a return to Astarte, Hera, Juno, Venus . . .? Sex goddesses, fertility goddesses, mother goddesses? . . . A resurrection of every ancient idolatry the Jewish idea came into the world to drive out, so as to begin again with the purifying clarity?[71]

She assumes the goddesses are sexual in a negative way. If Abraham's vision was "cleansing" then it came to replace something dirty.

Another assumption is that goddess worship was by definition polytheistic, since the goddess functioned as the consort of a male god. Western religious culture asserts that a god without a goddess is better, a higher, more noble idea. For example, in his decisive commentary on the Torah, Rabbi W. Gunther Plaut notes in his introduction,

> Comparison reveals similarities between biblical writings and other old Near Eastern sources, but it also reveals striking dissimilarities . . . There is no other ancient writing which approaches the Torah in its lofty concept of a unique God, who is not subject to fate or destiny, has no female consort, and is concerned with the welfare of all humanity.[72]

A god without a female consort—a male god, we can assume, since it/he has no female counterpart—is loftier than what came before. Even the use of the word "consort" is clear: A goddess is a kind of female companion, an escort or a lover.

What do we really know of paganism? What do we know that is truly and historically verifiable, other than what has been received and filtered through our own Western Judeo-Christian biases? We use the same epithet—"pagan," with a negative connotation—against Native religions, against Eastern religions, and against almost anything that does not resemble the Western Judeo-Christian formulation. Today's Wicca and other neo-pagan religions may have something in common with ancient worship, but we have very little documentation, and almost no records are left of how ancient cultures practiced paganism. It is hard to know how close they actually are, or how helpful they can be in explaining what our ancestors experienced.

Scholars studying pre-biblical religion come with their own prejudices and preconceptions. There exists little neutral scholarship on paganism. Charles Muses writes,

> Whenever the theme of goddess arises in a still male-dominated culture such as our global one today, there is an inevitable sexual reaction on the part of that culture and of male commentators in particular—a reaction that does not desist even from unscholarly smirking and besmirching, with consequent denigrating effect.[73]

The use of the word "cult" for the ceremonies of the early religions, for example, plants in the reader's mind an evil idolatry. Commonly accepted terminology like "cult prostitutes" for priestesses, and "orgies" for festivals make it nearly impossible to study in an unbiased way what the Torah was railing against, and why. If we approached the question of paganism and the goddess without the preconceived notion that they are evil, what might we find? If we do not automatically reject paganism as impure, assume that goddess worship included human sacrifices and other abominations, or instinctively associate the feminine divine with sexuality and nature, what might we uncover?

There is a temptation to ascribe to historical goddess-worshipping societies the kind of peace, harmony and gender equality we would like to see in our own. Scholars debate whether that view has historical veracity. But on the other hand, the image of the goddess provides a welcome relief from the dominant patriarchal images of mainstream Judaism.

The Torah has been expurgated not only of goddesses, but of any vestiges of the ancient ways, leaving only hints of what was: sacred trees and groves, magic circles, and the sacred pillars called in Hebrew *asherot*. That they were never completely erased from the texts points to their popularity and the indelible mark they left on the people. This accidental record of our forefathers and foremothers' attachment to the plurality of divine images, with their femininity and their sexuality, shows us the depth of their spiritual needs. They seem as unsatisfied with the one-sided maleness of God as we are.

The Torah has evidence of earlier practices, shifts from them and longings for them, along with tirades against them. Some of our ancestors in Israel must have continued to worship other gods and goddesses alongside YHVH, or why the need to totally destroy those sacred pillars—the *asherot*—in Deuteronomy 16? If they posed no threat to the structure of the new way, if the people were repulsed by them, uninterested in them, and repudiated them themselves, why destroy them? Clearly, they did still have power, and so to create solidarity in the Hebrew nation in a time of attack, and to ensure a new hierarchical and priestly social order, the Torah describes the rites of the neighboring nations as repugnant, their gods as useless, and their myths as supplanted by superior legends. But not with total success.

If we examine the places where censoring may have taken place, and where hints can still be discerned, we can ask with as little bias as possible: Is what we find usable, retrievable or transferable? Can we reappropriate it within a monotheistic rabbinic Judaism, or will it destroy that system?

Asherot: Sacred Trees, Sacred Posts and Goddesses

> These are the laws and rules which you must carefully observe in the land that the Lord, God of your fathers, is giving you to possess, as long as you live on the earth: you must destroy all the sites at which the nations you are to possess worshipped their gods, whether on lofty mountains and on hills or under any luxuriant tree. Tear down their altars, smash their pillars, put their sacred posts [*asherot*] to the fire, and cut down their images of the gods, obliterating their name from that site. Do not worship Adonai your God in like manner . . .
> (Deuteronomy 12: 1–4)

The word in the Torah most closely associated with a goddess or goddess worship is *asherah*. The Hebrew word *asherah* (in the plural *asherot*) appears in the Torah as a "sacred post" used by the surrounding peoples in their worship. It is to be consigned to the fire, along with their altars, pillars and images. Cones, pillars of stone, wooden pillars and trees were frequently found as emblems of the moon, on the sacred stones of the moon goddess.[74] The moon goddess whose worship spread farthest and who was most revered was named Ishtar in Babylonia, and known in Canaan as Astarte. Since the Hebrews lived in such close proximity to the Canaanites, it is likely that Astarte becomes *asherah* in Hebrew, no longer a proper name but now an object. The Torah reassigns Astarte's role to YHVH.

In Canaan, Astarte was known as the Mother of All and Opener of the Womb. In the Torah, the role of mother who creates all life is assigned to Eve. Now that we have a human "mother of all life," it makes sense to have a Father God, a male Divine creator. The Torah assigns the job of opening the womb to YHVH, who first opens Leah's womb (Genesis 29: 31), then Rachel's (Genesis 30: 22). In Exodus 13 we pledge the firstborn—that which opens the womb—to God. As the Canaanites gave honor to Astarte for opening women's wombs, the Torah designates honor to God who opens the womb. We have to "pay God back" with the opening of our wombs. YHVH, not Astarte, is the Hebrews' Opener of the Womb.

In Babylonian myth, Ishtar ruled over the cycles of the moon with her son Tammuz, who died at the turn of the year (summer solstice) and returned again for the harvest. At his "death" each year, the priestesses held a mourning festival, in which hymns of lamentation and wailing were performed by women throughout the land. Obviously these ceremonials maintained their attractiveness in the First Temple period, when women had not yet given up all connection to the goddess, for in Ezekiel 8: 14 we have a clear reference to Hebrew women in the inner court or north gate of the Temple participating in this festival of mourning for Tammuz. The traditional fast day of the 17th of Tammuz, declared by the rabbis a day of fasting and lamentation, calls to mind a reappropriation of the ancient custom of participation in the lamentation for Tammuz the god, practiced despite the condemnation of the earlier prophets.

The proper name of the goddess Astarte becomes in Hebrew the word for symbols previously associated with her. *Asherot* or sacred pillars are associated with trees. Abraham travels to the terebinths of Moreh, translated as the tree of "teaching" or "oracle," and circumcises himself near the terebinths of Mamre (Genesis 17). In Hebrew terebinth is *elah* and we note the similarity to *el*, meaning god, now taking a feminized form with an *ah* ending.

The "luxuriant trees" of Deuteronomy 12 are sites of worship. The Deuteronomy text also decrees that the sites upon "high mountains" where they worshipped are also to be destroyed. Perhaps that explains why Mount Sinai is never focal except for the brief moment in Exodus 19 at the giving of the Ten Commandments. Though the mountain shakes and quakes, it is from the Voice of God and not from the sacredness of the mountain itself. The Torah purposely assigns no special status to mountains, to differentiate Israel from the pagans who do. That is also why the building of the Tabernacle is so important. Deuteronomy 12 continues, "Do not worship the Lord your God in like manner, but look only to the site that the Lord your God will choose amidst all your tribes as His habitation, to establish His name there." Since the gods and goddesses of the ancient world all had their particular "homes"—and since the goddess was also revered outdoors in groves, among the trees—the Israelites needed to construct a structure dedicated to their own god, removed from the outdoor tree settings of the goddess.

Stones and pillars are to be destroyed except where they are detached from previous pagan meaning. Thus, in Deuteronomy 27: 17, stones used to demarcate borders between pieces of land, owned presumably by men, may not be destroyed.

Priestesses

We know that goddess worship involved priestesses. Yet we find no reference in the entire Torah to female priests. The Torah restricts this office to men, men "without blemish." Two types of priests functioned at the Tabernacle: the *cohanim*, or priests who offered the sacrifices, and Levites, assistants to the *cohanim* whose main functions included tending to the tabernacle and the *ner tamid*, the eternal flame on the altar. The Levites were to keep a perpetual fire burning.

There is a correlation between the Torah's Levites and the priestesses of the goddess. The main function of the priestesses of the goddess was also to tend sacred uninterrupted fires. In many temples of the moon goddess, a perpetual fire was tended by a group of priestesses dedicated to its service. The fertilizing power of the moon was symbolized by that light. Torches, candles and fires were burned to honor the moon and carried around fields to promote their fertility. The moon goddess was associated with fire. Ancient statues of the goddess Diana show her crowned with a crescent moon and carrying a torch. In her temple, priestesses maintained the eternal flame, extinguishing it only on "evil" days or taboo days, when the deity left the world of the living. It's interesting that the Torah prohibits the kindling of fire on the Sabbath, God's rest day, the day that God "withdraws" from the work of creation.

Unlike the Levites, the priestesses remained unmarried, and in some cases, performed sexual initiation rites with men desiring union with the goddess. Pledged to bringing the fertilizing power of the goddess into contact with humanity, they could neither wed nor enjoy sexual union with husbands or lovers; rather, they saved their sexuality for ritual purposes. They remained "virgins" in the sense that they never married common men.

The Torah calls such a priestess *kadesha*. Coming from the root *k-d-sh*, it means "holy one" or "sanctified one," but is most often translated into English as "cult prostitute." Prostitute is a misnomer, for they did not employ themselves as sexual objects for their own sustenance or in response to a social demand. They were employed to have sex with men in temple rituals, and their wages went into the running and functioning of that temple. This custom is strictly prohibited by the Torah in Deuteronomy 23, which states, "No Israelite woman shall be a *kadesha*, and no Israelite man shall be a *kadesh*. You shall not bring the fee of such a whore or a dog into the congregation of the Lord." The second part of the verse uses the common "street-walker" term *zonah* for whore, and *dog* for male prostitute. "Dog" may function here as common slang for a transvestite priest. Graves and Patai describe a yearly ritual between male worshippers and "dog-priests" dressed as women in the Hierapolis temple.[75]

The word "prostitute" instead of "priestess" creates a strong visceral predisposition against them. But it could be that even in the Hebrew the word *kadesha* is used sarcastically, as if to say only the pagans would consider such women holy. While the Torah rejects all recognition of their service, and vilifies the *kadesha* throughout the Torah, the occupation of these men and women was not considered to be immoral or reproachable in their own non-Hebrew society; on the contrary, they carried great honor. The Torah was deeply fearful of this kind of sexual ritual, and forbade the wages of such sexual activities to be used or reappropriated in service to YHVH. And just to be sure, all priestly power, especially the power to "tend the sacred fires," was now transferred to male Levites.

Male priests of the goddess also played a central role. Dedicated to serve a feminine god for life, they were expected to adopt feminine attributes. Thus they became eunuchs and wore feminine garb. Zealous helpers of Ishtar or Astarte often castrated themselves in ecstatic fits of frenzy. In Anatolia and Rome, young male devotees would take a "sacred knife" to their own body and run through the streets holding the severed parts. Custom decreed that they would fling the part into a house, and the inhabitants of that house would have to provide the new initiate with women's clothing.[76]

When describing the priests of YHVH, the Torah has to differentiate our priests from "their" priests. Thus no "blemished" man or any man with crushed testes can serve as a *cohen*, or priest of YHVH. Furthermore, no castrated man may even enter the "congregation of the Lord." This would certainly serve as a litmus test of whether he had been involved with the goddess cult. No man, priest or otherwise, is allowed to put on a woman's clothing, lest there be confusion between goddess worshippers, who followed such customs, and worshippers of YHVH.[77]

The Moon

Modern Jewish feminists have found new meaning in the association of women and the moon. Rosh Chodesh, the new month, has become popular as a time for special ceremonies marking our femaleness. Rosh Chodesh groups study and mark the connections between women and the moon, between our menstrual cycles and the moon's cycles, and between the ancient symbols of the moon and the symbols of femininity. This modern link has ancient origins.

Early civilizations saw the moon as having influence over fertility, and later revered it as a deity. The full moon, offering new hope and new life, was signalled with shouts and blasts of joy from royal trumpets similar to the Hebrew shofar, or ram's horn.

The waning moon represented the powers of destruction and death. Ancient societies equated the monthly cycle of women with the monthly cycle of the moon, and its "swelling" as her "swelling" in pregnancy.

Yet the Hebrew new month, also heralded by shofar blasts, takes place not on the full moon but on the last day of the old month and the first day of the new month. Both are the darkest days of the cycle. The Hebrew "new moon" is in fact the darkest night, or the "no moon." The ancient Hebrews blessed the moon at its darkest period, when its power is least evident, when it was specifically *not* worshipped by other cultures, when its femaleness, swelling, fullness, roundness, is absent. The power of the moon, connected to women, is negated in the darkness.

Our ancestors were familiar with both sun and moon cults. Sun cults, proliferating in Egypt and thus something our ancestors had seen and known, were in the hands of men. The Hebrews rejected the sun cults and their association with Egypt by counting the Hebrew calendar through the moon, not the sun. But by doing so, they acknowledged the powerful emotional tug of the feminine element in time. Moon cults were in the hands of women, and Hebrew women were also familiar with the reverent associations of the moon and femininity. Worship of the moon is one of the oldest forms of goddess worship. Cones or other figures of the moon goddess have even been found at the site of Mount Sinai.[78]

So the later Rabbis of the Talmud invented a midrash to explain, make acceptable and Judaize the already acknowledged pagan connection of women and the moon. In effect, through this midrash, they authorized women to celebrate what they probably had already been celebrating anyway. They taught that women were rewarded with Rosh Chodesh for refusing to participate in the building of the golden calf. Even today Rosh Chodesh is, for Orthodox women as well as those not Orthodox, a women's holiday on which women are commanded to rest and rejoice.[79]

The prophets denounced goddess worship, and especially opposed any such worship occurring at the time of the new moon or on the Sabbath (Jeremiah 44). They feared a symbiosis of pagan notions and Hebrew notions, a symbiosis that may have been occurring already among women. Perhaps women found worship of the goddess especially meaningful during the new moon, associating it with both menstrual and moon cycles. Or perhaps they knew of a connection between moon worship, menstruation and the Sabbath from very early pagan sources.

Such a link has been suggested by M. Esther Harding in her book *Woman's Mysteries*, in which she noted that the word *sabbatu* comes from *sa-bat* and means heart-rest. Thus it denotes the day of rest that the full moon takes when it appears to be neither increasing nor decreasing. On this day, it was considered unlucky to do any work, eat cooked food, or go on a journey. These things were also prohibited to the menstruating woman, and those taboos were extended to all on that day, the Sabbath, which at first was only observed once a month. Later, it became established at the beginning of each of the moon's four phases. She concludes,

> The Babylonian *sabbatu* was the "evil day" of the moon goddess Ishtar, when it is not unlikely that she was thought to be menstruating . . . it is strange to us to think that the prohibitions connected with "sabbath observance" are, in their far-off origins, menstrual taboos connected with the belief that the moon herself is a woman having a monthly period and sickness.[80]

Her followers called the moon goddess the goddess of renewal. She dies and is reborn as women are renewed each month. Prayers to her for renewal are still intoned by Native people. In the Jewish prayerbook, it is God who renews the moon, and not the moon who renews herself. But as it says in the prayers for Rosh Chodesh, "in the time to come, they [humankind] will be renewed like it."[81]

Rosh Chodesh, represents an authentically Jewish practice, with roots in paganism, which has been successfully reappropriated by Jewish feminists. It gives us an opportunity to see ourselves as linked to other women, to our menstrual cycles, to nature and to history all at the same time. As Robin Zeigler writes,

> Rosh Chodesh, the waxing and waning of the moon, speaks to my feminine tasks. I must remind myself that my life is filled with constant change. My body, whether pregnant, birthing, breast-feeding, or menstruating, is constantly changing. My reality is to learn to live with these changes—to ebb and flow with them . . .[82]

The Place of the Goddess and Shekhinah in Judaism

Some scholars have held the Hebrews responsible for all of patriarchy. They suggest that in the "good old goddess-worshipping days" peace and harmony abounded, until the Hebrews came along with their male YHVH, and everything went wrong. The covert anti-Semitism in this argument frightens feminists who still hold the Torah as containing the sacred history of the Jews, a link to our identity, and a record of our struggle to connect with the Divine. Words such as "patriarchal invaders" appear again and again in the writings of authors such as Merlin Stone. At least she admits that the Hebrews were not alone in their male-centeredness. She argues that the ancient cultures most influential upon the Hebrews, those of the Sumerians, Babylonians, Hittites and Canaanites, will "reveal . . . the murder of the goddess . . . the patriarchal attitudes of the Hebrews may have been formed, not in a cultural vacuum, as is generally assumed, but by their connections to the male-oriented northern invaders."[83]

On the one hand, I am not prepared to say the Torah is merely a systematic program to murder the goddess and violently impose male rule on all her followers. I still see in the Torah strong and valuable role models in both the matriarchs and patriarchs. I still see in the Torah a fundamental equality in God's eyes of male and female, even if that was not translated into the social strata of the day. I still see in the Torah lofty teachings of ultimate justice, ethical truisms and a blueprint for *tikkun olam*, making the world a better place. If the dominant image of God in the Torah is male, and human male privilege is secured by that image, I will still try to "fix" that image and its implications, because I believe that the Torah is more than a historical diary of the forced infiltration of patriarchy.

But, on the other hand, I am not prepared to ignore the implications of the discoveries of the previous paragraphs. Our distant ancestors obviously found great meaning in woman-identified worship, judging from how hard it was for them to let it go, and how strenuously the prophets and the Bible itself fought against such worship. They cared deeply about fecundity, fertility and reproduction, and needed poetic and religious expressions for that concern. They saw these as manifestations of Divine beneficence. Expressions that found their way into the Torah as blessings of the land abound, testifying to the centrality of fertility, even while the fertility-centered cults, with their associations of the land and the goddess, were being squashed. These blessings of the land are phrased in the language of female physicality. For example, Jacob, in the name of God, promises the Israelites "blessings of the breast and of the womb" in Genesis 49: 25.

As feminists, we are intrigued by what the *symbolism* of the goddess, if not the goddess herself, can hold for us. Scholars still debate whether those societies that worshipped the goddess did indeed ensure peace and wholeness for women. They question whether societies in which women held social status equal or even superior to that of men based that status on the worship of goddesses. Merlin Stone asserts that goddess worship was closely associated with matrilineal inheritance. Thus power and the bargaining position that comes with the ownership of property or title are assigned to women in those societies. Women had economic independence, and in some cases, significant sexual freedom, even if married.[84]

Contrast this with Tikva Frymer-Kensky's assertion that the goddesses

> . . . were not enshrined in a religion of women, but in the official religion of male-dominated societies; [they] . . . served as an integral part of a religious system that mirrored and provided the sacred underpinnings of patriarchy . . . the religion of Israel's contemporaries was not one in which gods and goddesses had equal roles and import . . . There was no longer possible a choice between monotheism and the goddess, but rather one between monotheism and a male-dominated polytheism.[85]

Thus, she suggests that Israelite monotheism actually *improved* the ancient world, whereas Stone believes it *destroyed* it. Frymer-Kensky states:

> The image of God must expand to include all the functions previously encompassed by an entire pantheon . . . The biblical system had to replace both goddesses and gods, and as it did so, it transformed its thinking about nature, culture, gender and humanity . . . Interaction among the gods is replaced by solo mastery, and humanity, divinity and cosmos have to be realigned.[86]

Relations between the gods, who had been seen as controlling nature and culture, no longer were the only deciding factor in whether it rained or not, or whether your crops failed. People now played a major role, in their exercising of the relationship between themselves and the One God. Instead of pitting one god against another, people could turn to the One God who would answer all their needs, if in return they showed loyalty to that One God.

Earthly fertility, as described in Genesis 1, now replaces the need for sexual union of male and female to ensure vegetation. The power to conceive is not a power possessed by either men or women, not dependent on supervision by a mother-goddess. Frymer-Kensky writes, "In this monotheistic view, all nature is one unified field. Everything is interrelated and under the control of one deity. In this organic view of the universe, there are no forces in tension and cooperation."[87]

Frymer-Kensky also reminds us that modern scholarship continues to question the validity of texts about ancient sexual practices in what she calls "the myth of orgy." There is little hard evidence, she claims, of the sexual initiation rites and the sexual role of priestesses apart from one mention in the story of Tamar and a prophetic mention of *kadeshot* weaving garments for Asherah. Our limited understanding of those so-called sexual rites is based on one ancient writer alone, Herodotus, whose intention was to prove the superiority of the Greeks over the "barbarians," about whose practices he wrote.[88]

Certainly the *symbolism* of the goddess holds some redemptive power for modern women. This symbolism becomes evident when we understand that a male godhead has historically been the highest form, the highest goal, and the highest aspiration of humanity. It is equally evident in modern attempts to posit a sexless god, whose Divinity transcends sexuality, offering humans that same level of spirituality only when devoid of their attachment to body.

The goddess helps reform the societal view that women's power is nonexistent or inferior, a threat to stability or a fad of the moment. As Carol Christ has written, the symbol of the goddess rids us of

> . . . the devaluation of female power, denigration of the female body, distrust of female will, and denial of the women's bonds and heritage that have been engendered by patriarchal religion. As women struggle to create a new culture in which women's power, body, will, and bonds are celebrated, it seems natural that the Goddess would reemerge as symbol of the newfound beauty, strength, and power of women.[89]

The goddess also has a "darker" side of fierceness, wildness and destruction. If we reappropriate goddess symbolism we will have to deal with these elements as well. As Judith Plaskow writes, "Unless the God who speaks to the feminist experiences of empowerment and connection can also speak to the frightening destructive and divisive aspects of our lives, a whole side of existence will be severed from the feminist account of the sacred.[90]"The images of the goddess—and the traditional images of God as creator of both light and darkness, life and death—speak to this wholeness.

There is a second direction we can turn for a feminine articulation of God. Reawakening the actual goddess aspects of YHVH, that is, incorporating goddess symbols for YHVH, who truly Encompasses All Things, can bring back women who feel that Judaism does not offer them a spirituality or a voice. Rabbi Lynn Gottlieb speaks of restoring the "... pre-biblical archetype of a female Creatrix to contemporary Jewish liturgy." Furthermore, she suggests that what we perceive as "traditional" Jewish symbols can be recast into their more ancient prototype, linking them specifically with a female aspect of the godhead. She states,

> ... Women continued to set up private altars in their homes as a way of expressing their need to connect through the symbols of their daily lives to a feminine Presence. This is the essence of the ritual around the Sabbath table wherein the use of candles, braided bread, and the liturgical image of the Sabbath Queen and Bride link Jewish women on an intuitive, if not explicit, level to the feminine divine.[91]

And, she suggests, by "remythologizing" Shekhinah, we can find already within Judaism a powerful feminine model.

The Hebrew name *Shekhinah* literally means "dwelling" and appears as a name for God's presence in rabbinic literature of the second century C.E. The midrash speaks of God placing "His Shekhinah" in the midst of Israel and of the Shekhinah resting upon individuals when they study Torah. Depicted often as luminous light, the Shekhinah shines with God's radiance. It is a manifestation of Divinity to indicate God's presence at a given place.

The later medieval Jewish philosophers described the Shekhinah as a separate entity itself, created by God. According to Judah Halevi, the Shekhinah dwelt first in the desert Tabernacle, then in the Temple; but when the Temple was destroyed the Shekhinah ceased to appear, and will only reappear with the coming of the Messiah.[92] With the development of the Kabbalah, Jewish mysticism, the Shekhinah takes on its definite feminine characteristics. In the late twelfth and thirteenth centuries C.E., the Shekhinah begins to be described as princess, daughter, and the feminine principle in the world. The Shekhinah is in exile along with the Jewish people; she reflects our state on a metaphoric level.

Jewish feminists have "rediscovered" Shekhinah. Venerated and exalted as the feminine godhead in many feminist circles, her name is used in prayer, meditation and ritual. Here we find a "traditional" Jewish image; she comes to us from the inside, not the outside. Here are our ancient goddess symbols—moon, mother, water, earth—all embodied in our own authentically Jewish symbol. Gottlieb writes, "The many images associated with the Shekhinah can become a source for women's encounter with the divine today as well as a bridge to our past. Women yearn for this possibility. When women speak of God She, we can finally picture ourselves as created in God's image."[93]

However, Shekhinah offers no complete answers and she is not a panacea. She is a projection of what male mystics believed femininity and the feminine principle in the world to be: passive and receptive. She occupies the lowest rung, the tenth and last of the *sephirot*, or divine emanations, that created the world. As such, she dwells the closest to earth, and closest to the "dark" powers. She has no light of her own, but receives the Divine light from the other *sephirot*. Because the Shekhinah contains so many facets of stereotypical female passivity, we will have to separate the traditional Kabbalistic Shekhinah from the Shekhinah we need and crave.

On a metaphoric level, however, Shekhinah holds tremendous power for us. The angels are her servants. She is the divine principle of the people Israel. She, together with Israel symbolizing the "wife" and God the "husband" replaces the goddess and yet remains part of the monotheistic vision of the One God. The Shekhinah is the closest first contact in the mystical struggle for communion with God. If, as the Kabbalists believed, the *mitzvot* (commandments) act as vehicles to reunite the masculine principle with the feminine, reharmonizing God and the Shekhinah who originally were One; and if Torah study and prayer bring a person into direct contact with her and thus with God, then the ultimate goal of Judaism is harmony.

We must look for harmony between God and Shekhinah, between masculine and feminine, and ultimately between male and female persons. As the Shekhinah and God are One, so too the masculine and feminine ultimately are also one, and need only be brought back together. We long to return to the Garden of Eden, to the one being both male and female, created in harmony and equality. We do so through daily acts that reunite the broken fragments of masculinity and femininity. If by bringing the Shekhinah "back" into mainstream Judaism we take one step toward that goal, toward restoring that time of peace and wholeness, we take an important and giant step.

Shekhinah, goddess, paganism—either redefined or as traditionally understood—all leave us with one fundamental question: Does monotheism as we have it now, as we have inherited it and continue to practice it, offer a sense of self-validation and self-esteem to women? Does it offer a renewed harmony between male and female?

The Jewish feminist task is one of symbiosis. It involves merging the old goddess imagery, the new ways of thinking about God, and the Kabbalistic notions of the Shekhinah with a rejection of stereotypical femininity; together with a staunch monotheism, an engagement with Rabbinic theologies and images of the Divine, and a respect for the ways in which all our early ancestors related to God. If our common Jewish notions of the One God can finally include feminine attributes, female pronouns, depictions of God as Mother and/or Father, descriptions of God as indwelling as well as being outside of us, if we can be bold, multifaceted and broad in our views, then the One God can yet be a symbol of the "newfound beauty, strength, and power of women."

God-Language

We spoke of the goddess aspect inherent in the One God, and of the Shekhinah having aspects which are attractive to the feminine soul. Now we close by asking about why, and how, we can speak of the One God in a more feminist manner.

When I was a little girl growing up in Queens, New York, my family would go to the Reform temple every Friday night. I would sit proudly in the front row. I loved the still serenity, the solemnity of the cantor's old European-style singing, and the sonorous tones of the rabbi's sermon. As I looked up at the *bima* (and from a little girl's vantage point, the *bima* looked very high up indeed), I thought surely God must be paying attention to all those deep and serious voices. When the rabbi invoked what he called the "final benediction," standing right in the middle of the *bima* with his arms spread out majestically, my father would put his hand on mine protectively and give it a little squeeze, his own silent blessing. I felt safe and secure with God the Father, the rabbi and my own father mysteriously intertwined.

Then I grew up. I found out that the rabbi was human, my father was flawed and God could not take care of everything. God as "He" does help re-create that safe and protective father of little boys and girls, but it lacks spiritual maturity.

God-language is not an academic discussion; nor is it a trivial matter, as some have suggested. Language can of course be poetic, esoteric, or symbolic in nature, but it is not arbitrary; language both *describes* and *creates* reality. While people rightly protest that symbols are not reality but only symbols, through centuries of familiarity, symbols lose their transparency and come to be seen as descriptive of, and not merely metaphors for, reality.

Language is not arbitrary. When we say table, we mean table, not chair. "Animal" is the generic term for certain creatures, but "cow" is specific. No one would argue that "cow" can also mean "chicken." How can we still argue then that He can also mean She? "God" is generic for that Being we try and describe, but "He" and "King" and "Father" are not.

Christian minister Sharon Neufer Emswiler once told of her experience in church, after years of singing hymns of the fatherhood of God and the brotherhood of men. She asked simply, "Why am I going away feeling less human than when I came?" If God is Father, and the Children of Israel are his "firstborn sons," then women are perpetually an other class, wives and mothers of those fathers and sons.

The representation of God in the Torah is predominantly male, expressed not only through the male pronoun, but through many male characteristics, such as God as a "man of war" (Exodus 15). Judith Plaskow writes,

> God's maleness is so deeply and firmly established as part of the Jewish conception of God that it is almost difficult to document: It is simply part of the lenses through which God is seen. Maleness is not a distinct attribute, separable from God's anger or mercy or justice. rather, it is expressed through the total picture of God in Jewish texts and liturgy.[94]

It is true that later Jewish philosophers, such as Maimonides, did champion an invisible, incorporeal God and rejected the anthropomorphism of the Torah as a projection of human need, noting that "the Torah speaks in a human language." But intertwined with that human, male language are issues of male dominance and male authority. If to be God-like is to be a Father and a King, a warrior and "Lord of hosts," and if to be God-like is the Jewish task of Imitatio Dei, then how can women ever be God-like? It is no accident that women do not experience themselves as equals within a society that encourages a masculine image for its highest divinity. And it is no accident that the highest source of our values, the ultimate model of holiness, the pinnacle of our search for meaning, is imagined in such male terms.

Plaskow further notes,

> If the feminist objections to Jewish God language were confined to the issues of gender, the manipulation of pronouns and creation of female imagery would fairly easily resolve the difficulties described . . . while feminist criticisms of traditional language begin with gender, they come to focus on the deeper issue of images of God's power as dominance.[95]

God's relationship to us is based on hierarchical opposites: father/son; king/servant; God is majestic, distant, exalted. This God is a Being utterly outside us, above, insisting on obedience and authority, punishing the wicked and rewarding the faithful.

Seen in this context, human male dominance makes sense, and is supported by the theological system as well as the legal system.

Language that envisions God as male or female correlates to the emergence of gender as a defining concern. What we say about God colors what we say about ourselves on a personal level. On a communal level, a religious society uses its theology to justify what women can/cannot and should/should not do within its social system. Thus God's maleness, a male priesthood, and the chosenness of "firstborn sons" all connect to a preoccupation with the rules, roles and rights of women. Feminism questions root assumptions and root beliefs about God and the resulting hierarchical nature of religion. It confronts root conceptions, and the root comfort, of God as Father.

If we are frightened to replace God the Father, it may be because we cannot imagine ritual, prayer, tradition and belief system with God the Partner. A male clergy will no longer be able to claim ultimate authority from a male God. Halacha, with all its assumptions about what women are and what women want, and what women can or cannot do, will have to deal with a new categories.

There are several ways to approach this new area of "God-talk" in an attempt to move away from a mostly male religious lexicon. We can change the language to include "She." The use of She helps point out the anthropomorphism and ultimate blasphemy of centuries of using He. If we never *really* meant that God was a "He," we should have no problem whatsoever using the term She. However, use of the term She provokes the old cries of paganism, although "He" never has. I have yet to hear that "He" is reminiscent of the old gods.

Or we can use neutral language. We can speak of God as "God" instead of either He *or* She. King becomes Ruler, Father becomes Parent. Such neutralization works only when the listeners divest themselves of all male stereotypes and archetypes so that the word "Parent" does not automatically conjure up a father. Neutral language only works when it doesn't let us hide our still-male imagery behind masks of neutrality. When we say Ruler, we still think King. Neutralizing the words does not always neutralize the effect of centuries of predominant images.

English, being a non-gendered language, is easy to change. We have to be more creative about Hebrew, which like French and other romance languages, is gendered. Marcia Falk has done groundbreaking work in her *Book of Blessings*, offering a new Hebrew, which speaks not only in a non-gendered way but also in a non-hierarchical way. No longer does she use the "Blessed Art Thou, Lord Our God, King of the Universe" formula; instead she suggests: "We bless the Source of Life." (The word "we" in Hebrew takes neither the male nor the female form, but is a truly "neutral" pronoun.) Rather than God remaining the distant King or becoming a Queen, God becomes the Core of Life, the Fountain of Life, and other more immanent (inner) rather than transcendent (outer) idioms. Her use of language moves the enterprise not only away from gender, but also away from traditional formulations of God as over us, reigning supreme, and demanding our praise.[96]

But neutral language has limitations, because we learn that we are created in God's image, and we ourselves are gendered beings. By degendering God we minimize our own human male and femaleness. We see humanity clearly in God's image when that imagery is both male and female, since we exist as male and female.

And we can add the little bit of female imagery that already exists. For example, God is called the Rock who gives birth (Deuteronomy 32), and in the same chapter the Rock is portrayed as an object of suckling. The prophet Isaiah speaks of God as a mother (Isaiah 42, 49 and 66). Job speaks of God's womb (Job 38).

Do we have to go outside the Torah to find the integration of maleness and femaleness in our description of God, or is there something, either obvious or hidden, in the Torah itself that can lead us in that direction? I find a starting point in the very oldest layers of Judaism and pre-biblical religion. I have to "re-vision" what the Torah had in mind when it shunned the goddess. I want to understand the fear of paganism and yet, in uncovering the layers of symbolism familiar to our ancestors, I try to "re-mythologize"[97] and create a new Jewish mythos, which includes the feminine aspects along with the masculine aspects of the One God.

Epilogue

It has been three years since I sat down to write this book, and I feel bolder than when I started. During that time, Dr. Marcia Falk revolutionized Jewish prayer with her new gender-inclusive, nonhierarchical Hebrew formulations in *The Book of Blessings*. Ellen Frankel opened up the world of women's Torah commentary, and a whole new way of formulating that commentary, with *The Five Books of Miriam*. Rabbi Debra Orenstein compiled and made public new women's rituals in *Lifecycles*. These three volumes represent just a sample of the proliferation of interest in and serious consideration of the spiritual needs of Jewish women now available. These new books make me feel brave, because they, too, are brave. They do not restate the old formulas in new, softer, feminine wrapping. They do not assume that Judaism already has all the answers, if only we look hard enough. They change form as well as content. They not only create new ways of seeing and telling, but normalize those new ways. The authors are bold new revisionists. I hope to stand among them.

I want to go farther than I have in the past. Over a decade ago, I participated in the documentary film *Half the Kingdom*. In the opening scene, I officiate at a baby-naming. I use all the traditional blessings, all the traditional forms, adding the matriarchs and including the mother and grandmother of the child in blessing the baby. If we were to make the film now, I would change the blessings altogether, sometimes using He, sometimes using She, sometimes finding a neutered term. I would use Marcia Falk's new forms along with the traditional ones. I would find some dramatic ritual, some way of marking the girl's entrance into the Jewish covenant with more than words. I would use more tactile elements. I would probably change the form *and* the content. Instead of showing me in my congregation marching with a Torah scroll, I would ask the producer to shoot scenes of my Rosh Chodesh group tying red strings around my pregnant belly and praying for an easy delivery. I would show the congregation joining me in chants using the name of Shekhinah, and doing a meditation before Neilah.

In its time, the film was considered very bold, and indeed it was. It opened a whole generation to the questions of the role of women in Judaism. But now, I would be even bolder.

I assume many of the readers of this book, each in his or her own way, has tried to answer the question posed in my introduction: How do we straddle the fence without losing our balance, with one foot in the feminist camp, and one foot in the Jewish camp; with one foot in modernity and the other foot in tradition?

While we maintain the balancing act, with as much grace as possible, many of us feel we are always fighting "the Jewish establishment." We are accused of thwarting more "important" or "urgent" issues, such as Israel or interdenominational unity. We are accused of being selfish and egotistical when we ask for more leadership roles, more women's issues in the main agenda, more attention to women's voices. We are asked to choose between Judaism and feminism, as if the two were adversaries. We are told to be patient, that our needs as women are secondary to "Jewish" needs.

We plant ourselves more firmly in the middle, or we jump off on one side or the other.

It is time to widen our Jewish feminist horizons and try things that may at first feel strange or unfamiliar. It is time to move beyond "equal access" Judaism, an egalitarian framework where women get to do the things men do, in much the same way as men. We need to move into bolder Judaism, a Judaism that takes chances, that tries new methods of praying, new incorporations of goddess and female imagery, new rituals of blood and water. We revision a Judaism that teaches and preaches the story of equality in Genesis 1. We move onto the bridge between Judaism and feminism not as a way-station, but as home. There we unpack and set down roots, in that intersection between the two loves.

I wish I could be completely optimistic, but I cannot. I work as one of the only female rabbis in Canada, a conservative and traditional community in all areas, but especially in the Jewish sector. As I write this, many of the Conservative congregations in Toronto still do not call adult women up to the Torah. (Girls can read from the scroll on the day of their Bat Mitzvah, but never again thereafter.) There are now two women in Toronto certified as a *mohalot* (ritual circumcisers), but they do not get the volume of calls their male colleagues do. I don't get counted in the *mezuman*, the three needed for the opening blessing of the grace after meals, at the Toronto Board of Rabbis, where I am supposedly a rabbi among colleagues. People wonder aloud if that union would fold, rather than allow a woman to be its president. The "old boys' network" is alive and well.

People still say, "Go slowly, give us time." It doesn't matter that I reply, "Five thousand years seems time enough, don't you think?" Congregations still worry about having too many women in leadership at the same time—rabbi, cantor, president. There has to be a man somewhere, for balance. Didn't anyone notice the imbalance when there was only one woman, or none? I still sit at rabbinic conferences with male colleagues who fear we are "taking over," as if there were a limited amount of power and, like toys in the playground, it may not be shared, because only one person or group can have it at a time. The Orthodox world, in the main, still fears, belittles and condemns Jewish feminism, rather than embracing its challenge as one of ultimate growth. Their voice is often the one heard in the secular world, as spokes*men* for "real" Judaism.

So we have to push forward, compassionate but unyielding to those who would rather wait behind. Let us take those who are ready with us, and, like Miriam, sing the rest of the Israelites across.

Chizki, chizki, v'nitchazek: be strong, and of good courage. Be bold.

Glossary

Akedah: Literally means "the binding." The *Akedah* refers to the story in Genesis 21, in which Abraham is called by God to bring his son Isaac up the mountain as an offering. At the last minute, Isaac is saved by Divine intervention.

Aliyah, plural *aliyot*: The honor of being called up to the Torah for the blessings before and after its reading. Called "having an *aliyah*."

Bar Mitzvah: A boy child's coming of age at thirteen, at which time he is permitted to have an *aliyah* and count in the *minyan*. *Bar Mitzvah* also refers to the ceremony which acknowledges this milestone, as in "I had a Bar Mitzvah."

Bat Mitzvah: A girl child's coming of age, traditionally at twelve, but acknowledged in the liberal communities at thirteen. Bat Mitzvah ceremonies began in the 1920s and exist now in almost all denominations in one form or another.

Bima: The platform in the synagogue from which services are led; usually the rabbi and cantor stand on the *bima*, as well as others who have service honors.

Bris: The Ashkenazic pronunciation of *brit*. See *brit*.

Brit: Literally means "covenant." God makes a *brit* with many biblical characters. Today we usually associate this word with the covenant of circumcision. See *brit milah*.

Brit milah: Literally "the covenant of circumcision." This ceremony is performed at eight days when the foreskin of the infant boy is removed amid blessings and ritual. Circumcision was commanded to Abraham as a "sign" of the covenant for all Jewish males for all time.

Cantor: The person responsible for the musical portions of a prayer service.

Cohen, plural *cohanim*: The highest priestly class, who served in the desert Tabernacle and then in the Temple in Jerusalem. Some people still trace their lineage to the *cohanim* of old, and these modern descendants receive the first *aliyah* in traditional synagogues, as a sign of honor and respect.

Halacha: The overall term for Jewish law, codified through the ages, since the Torah. *Halacha* is still evolving, in all the denominations.

Halachists: Experts in *halacha*.

Kabbalah: Jewish mysticism, developed throughout the ages but mostly associated with the system popularized in the thirteenth century C.E., in the town of Safed in Israel.

Kabbalists: Those who practice *Kabbalah*.

Kaddish: The memorial prayer, said for eleven months after a blood relative passes away. Traditionally, only men say this prayer, for deceased women and men. In liberal communities it is common for women to say the *Kaddish* for their loved ones.

Ketubah, plural *ketubot*: A Jewish wedding certificate, stipulating the promises made by the groom and bride, including material sustenance and sexual satisfaction. The traditional *ketubah* has the groom acquiring the bride for a price. Egalitarian *ketubot* are being written and used today, as well.

Levites: Assistants to the priests, they were honored servants of the sacred rites in the desert Tabernacle and then in the Temple in Jerusalem. Those people who still trace their lineage to the Levites of old receive the second *aliyah* in a traditional synagogue.

Mezuman: A quorum of three adults needed in order to include the introductory sections of the grace after meals. Traditionally, only men count in the *mezuman*; in liberal congregations and gatherings women count as well.

Midrash, plural *midrashim*: A Rabbinic story, parable or interpretation of biblical text, coming from the root *d-r-sh*, which means "to examine." These *midrashim* help fill in gaps in the text, supply missing details or dialogue, and enliven the text with personal anecdotes. Early *midrashim* can be found in the Talmud, from the second century, but the first actual compendia were edited in the fifth and sixth centuries C.E. Modern *midrashim* are still being written today.

Midrashist: Those involved in the writing or creating of *midrashim*.

Mikraot Gedolot: A page of Torah text surrounded by various commentaries, all in Hebrew. Commonly studied in advanced classes and in seminary.

Mikveh, plural *mikvaot*: A pool of water used for ritual immersions. Containing both natural rain water and tap water, built and filled to exact legal specifications, *mikvaot* are used traditionally to immerse new dishes, brides (and in some cases grooms), converts to Judaism, and women after their monthly menstrual period. Separate *mikvaot* are used to immerse corpses for final purification before burial.

Minyan: A quorum of ten needed for public prayers. In Orthodox services, only men are counted in the ten. In liberal services, either women or men or both together are counted in the ten.

Mitzvah, plural *mitzvot*: A commandment from the Torah, or later a commandment enacted by the rabbis.

Mohel: A Jew trained in the specific ritual of *brit milah*. The feminine form is *mohelet*. Feminine plural *mohalot*.

Ner Tamid: The eternal light that is kept above the ark in all synagogues, regardless of denomination. This light is on for all services, and, in some synagogues, is kept lit all the time. It is a memorial to the fire that was kept burning all the time in the Temple in Jerusalem in biblical days.

Neshama: Literally, "soul."

Niddah: The state of being in menstruation; also refers to the woman herself when menstruating. In the traditional community, there are very strict rules governing both the woman and those around her during that time.

Sephirot: According to *Kabbalists*, there were ten "vessels" or Divine emanations that issued from God during the creation of the world. Those ten *Sephirot* are used to explain everything from the existence of evil to the nature of God in the *Kabbalah*.

Shabbat: The Jewish Sabbath, beginning Friday at sundown and lasting until Saturday at sundown.

Sheloshim: The thirty-day mourning period for a blood relative following the burial.

Simchat Torah: The fall festival of rejoicing in the Torah, during which Jews dance with the scrolls, finish reading the book of Deuteronomy and then begin at Genesis again.

Succot: The fall festival of Booths, during which Jews eat—and some sleep—in fragile huts for eight or seven days, depending on the community. The huts, called *succah* in the singular, are reminders of the booths the Jews lived in during the forty years of wandering in the desert. Sometimes spelled *sukkah* and *sukkot*.

Taharah: Literally, "purity." The state of being that a person or object enters after immersion in the *mikveh*. In Temple times, only persons in this state were allowed to participate in ritual activities.

Tallis: Ashkenazic pronunciation of *tallit*. See *tallit*.

Tallit: A prayer shawl worn during daytime services, and once a year at night on Yom Kippur. Women have begun making and wearing the *tallit* in recent times.

Talmud: The compilation of Rabbinic law, comprising the *Mishnah* (legal decisions edited in the third century C.E.) and the *Gemara* (Rabbinic discussions of those laws, edited in the sixth century C.E.). In the traditional community, the *Talmud* is authoritative on matters of daily life.

Tanach (TNK): An acrostic for the whole of the Jewish Bible, which is divided into three sections: *T*orah (Five Books of Moses), *N*eviim (Prophets) and *K*etuvim (Writings.)

Terebinth: A small Mediterranean tree with winged leaves.

Tevilah: Immersion in the *mikveh*.

Tumah: Literally "impurity." In Temple times, a person in this state was not permitted to participate in ritual activities. *Tumah* is contracted from contact with untouchable or unapproachable persons or objects, such as corpses.

Yeshivah: A school of full-time Jewish learning for either children or adults.

YHVH: The four-letter Hebrew name of God, composed of the Hebrew letters *yud-hey-vav-heh*, commonly pronounced "Adonai." It is not known how those four letters were actually pronounced in the days of the Torah.

NOTES

Introduction

1. Joseph Campbell and Charles Muses, eds., *In All Her Names* (New York: Harper San Francisco, 1991), 19.
2. Naomi Goldenberg, *Changing of the Gods* (Boston: Beacon Press, 1979), 10, 13, 22.
3. Norma Rosen, "Rebecca and Isaac: A Marriage Made in Heaven," in *Out of the Garden: Women Writers on the Bible*, Christina Buchmann and Celina Spiegel, eds. (New York: Fawcett Columbine, 1994), 24–25.
4. See the modern midrash in *Taking the Fruit* (Chico, CA: Women's Institute for Continuing Jewish Education, 1981), 21.
5. Mary Ann Tolbert, "Defining the Problem: The Bible and Feminist Hermeneutics," in *Semeia*, vol. 28 (1983): 122.
6. For an excellent analysis of this idea, see Tikva Frymer-Kensky's article "The Bible and Women's Studies" in *Feminist Perspectives on Jewish Studies*, Lynn Davidman and Shelly Tenenbaum, eds. (New Haven: Yale University Press, 1994), especially page 23.
7. Tolbert, "Defining the Problem: The Bible and Feminist Hermeneutics," 121.
8. Carol A. Newsome and Sharon H. Ringe, eds., *The Women's Bible Commentary* (Louisville, KY: Westminster/John Knox Press, 1992), 151.

Part I

9. Paula Cooey, "The Power of Transformation and the Transformation of Power," in *Journal of Feminist Studies in Religion*, vol. I, no. 1: 28, n. 14.
10. Ibid., 36.
11. Newsome and Ringe, eds., *The Women's Bible Commentary*, 3–4.
12. J.A. Phillips, *Eve: The History of an Idea* (San Francisco: Harper and Row, 1984), 12–13.
13. As quoted in W. Gunther Plaut, ed., *The Torah: A Modern Commentary* (New York: Union of American Hebrew Congregations, 1981), 33, citing Phyllis Trible, "From Depatriarchalizing in Biblical Interpretation," in *Journal of the American Academy of Religion*, vol. 41, no. 1 (March 1973): 30–48.

14. Bereshit Rabbah 18, Devarim Rabbah 6, and Tanhuma Vayeshev.

15. Talmud, tractate Yevamot 65b, states that the mitzvah is incumbent upon those who are commanded to subdue, not upon those commanded to be subdued. In the Midrash, Genesis Rabbah 8:14, the rabbis suggest that if women were commanded to bear children, they might sin through good intentions; that is, "that she not go seeking in the marketplace."

16. See, for example, Leila Leah Bronner, *From Eve to Esther* (Louisville, KY: Westminster/John Knox Press, 1994), 41, n. 40.

17. The legend of Lilith takes many forms. It can be found, for example, in the Zohar I, 19b; in Louis Ginzberg, *The Legends of the Jews* (Philadelphia: Jewish Publication Society of America, 1909), vol. I, 65, and vol. V, 87–89; J.D. Eisenstein, ed., *Otzar Midrashim* (New York: J.D. Eisenstein, 1915), vol. I. There is no "original" source since the legend is ancient and has pre-Hebrew origins, but one of the earliest mentions is in the Alphabet of Ben Sira, where she is identified as "the first Eve." For a full discussion of the Lilith legend, see Barbara Black Koltuv, *The Book of Lilith* (York Beach, ME: Nicolas-Hays, 1987) or *The Encyclopedia Judaica* (Jerusalem: Keter, 1972), vol. 11, under "Lilith."

18. Phillips, *Eve: The History of an Idea*, 4.

19. Sharon Pace Jeansonne, *The Women of Genesis* (Minneapolis: Fortress Press, 1990), 72.

20. Talmud, tractate Baba Batra 123a.

21. Introduction to Eicha Rabba; also in Yalkut Shimoni Eicha.

22. Jeansonne, *The Women of Genesis*, 78.

23. Ilana Pardes, *Countertraditions in the Bible* (Cambridge, MA: Harvard University Press, 1992), 67.

24. See her book *In a Different Voice* (Cambridge, MA: Harvard University Press, 1982), ch. 2.

25. See Nahum Sarna, ed., *The JPS Torah Commentary: Exodus* (Philadelphia: Jewish Publication Society, 1991) 7, n. 15.

26. Talmud, tractate Sotah, pages 12b and 13a; also Shemot Rabbah:1.

27. Talmud, tractate Ta'anit 9a.

28. Sarna, ed., *The JPS Torah Commentary: Exodus*, 10, n. 7–10.

29. Louis Ginzberg, *The Legends of the Jews* (Philadelphia: Jewish Publication Society of America: 1909), 290

30. Sarna, ed., *The JPS Torah Commentary: Exodus*, 24–26.

31. Numbers Rabbah 21:10.

32. Neusner notes that ancient Sumerian law allowed unmarried daughters to inherit; and that Nuzi and Ugarit documents make it clear that daughters inherit in the absence of sons. See Sarna, ed., *The JPS Torah Commentary: Numbers*, 482.

33. Talmud, tractate Baba Batra 120a.

34. Ibid.

Part II

35. Elizabeth Dodson Gray, ed., *Sacred Dimensions of Women's Experience* (Wellesley, MA: Roundtable Press 1988), 197.

36. For a full discussion of Judaism and sexuality, see under "Sexuality" in *The Encyclopedia Judaica*, or David Feldman, *Birth Control in Jewish Law* (New York: New York University Press, 1968).

37. Mary Douglas, *Purity and Danger* (London: Routledge and Kegan Paul, 1966), 120.

38. Aryeh Kaplan, *Waters of Eden: The Mystery of the Mikveh* (New York: NCSY/Union of Orthodox Jewish Congregations, 1976), 14.

39. Some recent examples can be found in Debra Orenstein, ed., *Lifecycles* (Woodstock, VT: Jewish Lights Publishing, 1994).

40. One of the strongest critics of a Jewish feminism that relies on the biological celebration of womanhood is Cynthia Ozick. See, for example, her chapter "Hannah and Elkanah: Torah as the Matrix of Feminism," in *Out of the Garden: Women Writers on the Bible*, Christina Buchmann and Celina Spiegel, eds. (New York: Fawcett Columbine, 1994). On page 91 she writes, "I speak of the idea of feminism as transcendence of biology . . . the urgency of classical feminism . . . was precisely the fight against the notion that anatomy was destiny."

41. See for example: S. Dresner, *The Jewish Dietary Laws: Their Meaning for Our Time* (New York: Burning Bush Press, 1959); Louis A. Berman, *Vegetarianism and the Jewish Tradition* (New York: Ktav, 1982); or Rav Kook quoted in Nehama Leibowitz, *Studies in Vayikra* (Jerusalem: World Zionist Organization, 1980), 55.

42. Herbert Chanan Brichto, "On Slaughter and Sacrifice, Blood and Atonement" in *Hebrew Union College Annual*, vol. 47, 1976, 22.

43. See Nehama Leibowitz, *Studies in Vayikra* (Jerusalem: World Zionist Organization, 1980), 51–56. For a description of "eating round the blood" and the use of a blood-bowl in goddess societies, see Erich Neumann, *The Great Mother* (Princeton, NJ: Princeton University Press, 1983), 287–289.

44. Newsome and Ringe, eds., *The Women's Bible Commentary*, 31.

45. Parts of this section originally appeared as my article "... who *has* made me a woman ..." in *Lilith Magazine*, Spring 1990.

46. Naomi R. Goldenberg, "Archetypal Theory and the Separation of Mind and Body," in *Weaving the Visions*, Judith Plaskow and Carol Christ, eds. (San Francisco: HarperCollins, 1989), 244.

47. Carole Christ and Judith Plaskow, eds., In *WomanSpirit Rising* (San Francisco: Harper and Row, 1979), 251.

48. Ibid., 252.

49. Neumann, *The Great Mother*, 290–291.

50. Tamar Frankiel, *The Voice of Sarah: Feminine Spirituality and Traditional Judaism* (San Francisco: Harper and Row 1990), 81–82.

51. Rachel Biale, *Women and Jewish Law* (New York: Schocken Books, 1984), 148.

52. Blu Greenberg, *On Women and Judaism: A View from Tradition* (Philadelphia: Jewish Publication Society, 1981), 118–120.

53. Mishnah Niddah 5:3.

54. Kaplan, *Waters of Eden*, 44.

55. Howard Eilberg-Schwartz, *The Savage in Judaism: An Anthropology of Israelite Religion and Ancient Judaism* (Bloomington and Indianapolis: Indiana University Press, 1990), 180.

56. Gary Shapiro, "Sealed in Our Flesh: Women as Members of the Brit," in *Pardes Revisited* (newsletter of the Pardes Institute). I am indebted to him for many of the ideas in this section.

57. Grey, ed., *Sacred Dimensions of Women's Experience*, 61.

58. Douglas, *Purity and Danger*, 115–16.

59. Maimonides, Guide for the Perplexed II:49.

60. "How to Deal with a Jewish Issue," Rabbi Zalmen Schacter-Shalomi, in *A Mentsch among Men*, Harry Brod, ed. (Freedom, CA: Crossing Press, 1988), 82.

61. Portions of this section originally appeared in my article "Take Back the Waters," in *Lilith Magazine*, no. 15, Summer 1986.

62. Yonah Klem, "No Ordinary Bath: The Use of the Mikveh in Healing from Incest," in *Jewish Women Speak Out: Expanding the Boundaries of Psychology*, Kayla Weiner and Arinna Moon, eds. (Seattle: Canopy Press, 1995), 129.

63. See my article "The Mikveh as Spiritual Therapy" in *Journal of Reform Judaism*, Central Conference of American Rabbis, Winter/Spring 1995.

64. Rachel Adler, "In Your Blood Live: ReVisions of a Theology of Purity," in *Tikkun*, vol. 8, no. 1 (Jan./Feb. 1993): 41.

Part III

65. Robert Graves and Raphael Patai, *Hebrew Myths* (New York: Doubleday, 1964), 26.

66. The serpent as a symbol of the goddess's oracular wisdom is ". . . still evidenced in historical times by the association of the serpent (python) with the high priestess (pythoness) who gave divinely inspired counsel to Greek heads of state at the famous oracular shrine at Delphi." Campbell and Muses, eds., *In All Her Names*, 12.

67. M. Esther Harding, *Woman's Mysteries* (New York: G.P. Putman and Sons, 1971), 54.

68. Graves and Patai, *Hebrew Myths*, 69 and 150.

69. Merlin Stone, *When God Was A Woman* (New York: Dial Press, 1976), 36–37.

70. Plaut, ed., *The Torah: A Modern Commentary*, 212.

71. Cynthia Ozick, "Notes toward Finding the Right Question" in *On Being a Jewish Feminist*, Susanna Heschel, ed. (New York: Schocken Books, 1983), 120–121.

72. Plaut, ed., *The Torah: A Modern Commentary*, xxxvi.

73. Campbell and Muses, eds., *In All Her Names*, 45.

74. Harding, *Woman's Mysteries*, 42.

75. Graves and Patai, *Hebrew Myths*, 169. See also Harding, *Woman's Mysteries*, 218.

76. Harding, *Woman's Mysteries*, 141–2.

77. See Deuteronomy 12, 16, and 23; 2 Kings 23 for a detailed account of the campaign to finally wipe out the goddess's male priesthood, destroy their special quarters and eradicate the popular worship of Astarte.

78. Harding, *Woman's Mysteries*, 41.

79. Pirke de Rebbe Eliezar 45; see also Talmud, tractate Megillah 22b. For more information on the history and modern interpretations of Rosh Chodesh and its celebrations, see Susan Berrin, ed., *Celebrating the New Moon: A Rosh Chodesh Anthology* (Northvale, NJ: Jason Aronson Inc., 1996).

80. Harding, *Woman's Mysteries*, 63.

81. Dr. Joseph H. Hertz, ed., *Authorized Daily Prayerbook* (New York: Bloch Publishing Company, 1957), 995.
82. Robin Zeigler, "My Body, My Self and Rosh Chodesh," in *Celebrating the New Moon: A Rosh Chodesh Anthology*, Susan Berrin, ed. (Northvale, NJ: Jason Aronson Inc., 1996), 38.
83. Ibid., 104.
84. Stone, *When God Was a Woman*, ch. 3.
85. Tikva Frymer-Kensky, *In the Wake of the Goddess* (New York: Free Press, 1992), vii and 6.
86. Ibid., 85 and 89.
87. Ibid., 98.
88. Ibid., ch. 18.
89. Carole Christ and Judith Plaskow, eds., *Woman Spirit Rising*, (San Francisco: Harper and Row, 1976), 286.
90. Judith Plaskow, "Facing the Ambiguity of God" in *Tikkun*, vol. 6, no. 5: 70.
91. Lynn Gottlieb, *She Who Dwells Within*, (San Francisco: HarperCollins, 1995), 7–9.
92. Kuzari, 2:20, 23; 3:23. For a more complete discussion of the Shekhinah in Jewish tradition, see *The Encyclopedia Judaica*, vol. 14, under "Shekhinah."
93. Gottlieb, *She Who Dwells Within*, 22.
94. Judith Plaskow, *Standing Again at Sinai* (San Francisco: Harper San Francisco, 1990), 123.
95. Ibid., 128.
96. See Marcia Falk, *Book of Blessings* (San Francisco: HarperCollins, 1996).
97. Rabbi Lynn Gottlieb coined this term in her book *She Who Dwells Within*.

Bibliography and Suggested Further Reading

Adler, Rachel. "In Your Blood, Live: ReVisions of a Theology of Purity." *Tikkun* magazine, vol. 8, no. 1, Jan./Feb. 1993.

Berrin, Susan, ed. *Celebrating the New Moon: A Rosh Chodesh Anthology*. Northvale, NJ: Jason Aronson, 1996.

Biale, Rachel. *Women and Jewish Law*. New York: Schocken Books, 1984.

Brichto, Herbert Chanan. "On Slaughter and Sacrifice, Blood and Atonement." *Hebrew Union College Annual*, vol. 47, 1976.

Brod, Harry, ed. *A Mentsch among Men*. Freedom, CA: Crossing Press, 1988.

Bronner, Leila Leah. *From Eve to Esther*. Louisville, KY: Westminster/John Knox Press, 1994.

Buchmann, Christina and Spiegel, Celina, eds. *Out of the Garden: Women Writers on the Bible*. New York: Fawcett Columbine, 1994.

Campbell, Joseph and Muses, Charles, eds. *In All Her Names*. San Francisco: Harper San Francisco, 1991.

Christ, Carole and Plaskow, Judith, eds. *WomanSpirit Rising*. San Francisco: Harper and Row, 1979.

Cooey, Paula. "The Power of Transformation and the Transformation of Power." *Journal of Feminist Studies in Religion*, vol. I, no. 1. Decatur, GA: Scholars Press, 1987.

Davidman, Lynn, and Tenenbaum, Shelly, eds. *Feminist Perspectives on Jewish Studies*. New Haven and London: Yale University Press, 1994.

Douglas, Mary. *Purity and Danger*. London: Routledge and Kegan Paul, 1966.

Eilberg-Schwartz, Howard. *God's Phallus and Other Problems for Men and Monotheism*. Boston: Beacon Press, 1994.

Eilberg-Schwartz, Howard. *The Savage in Judaism: An Anthropology of Israelite Religion and Ancient Judaism*. Bloomington and Indianapolis: Indiana University Press, 1990.

Falk, Marcia. *The Book of Blessings*. San Francisco: HarperCollins, 1996.

Frankel, Ellen. *The Five Books of Miriam*. New York: G.P. Putnam's Sons, 1996.

Frymer-Kensky, Tikva. *In the Wake of the Goddess*. New York: MacMillan, 1992.

Fuchs, Esther. "Structure and Patriarchal Functions in the Biblical Betrothal Type-Scene: Some Preliminary Notes." *Journal of Feminist Studies in Religion*, vol. 3, no. 1, Spring 1987.

Frankiel, Tamar. *The Voice of Sarah: Feminine Spirituality and Traditional Judaism*. San Francisco: Harper and Row, 1990.

Gilligan, Carole. *In a Different Voice*. Cambridge, MA: Harvard University Press, 1982.

Ginzberg, Louis. *The Legends of the Jews*. Philadelphia: Jewish Publication Society of America, 1909.

Goldenberg, Naomi R. *Changing of the Gods*. Boston: Beacon Press, 1979.

Goldstein, David. *Jewish Mythology*. Northants, England: Hamlyn Publishing Group, 1987.

Goldstein, Elyse. "The Mikveh as Spiritual Therapy," *Journal of Reform Judaism*, Central Conference of American Rabbis, Winter/Spring 1995.

Goldstein, Elyse. "Take Back the Waters," *Lilith Magazine*, no. 15, Summer 1986.

Goldstein, Elyse. ". . . who *has* made me a woman . . ." *Lilith Magazine*, vol. 15, no. 2, Spring 1990.

Gottlieb, Lynn. *She Who Dwells Within*. San Francisco: Harper San Francisco, 1995.

Graves, Robert. *The White Goddess*. London: Faber and Faber, 1961.

Graves, Robert and Patai, Raphael. *Hebrew Myths*. Garden City, NY: Doubleday and Co., 1964.

Gray, William G. *Evoking the Primal Goddess*. St. Paul, MN: Llewellyn Publishing, 1989.

Gray, Elizabeth Dodson, ed. *Sacred Dimensions of Women's Experience*. Wellesley, MA: Roundtable Press, 1988.

Greenberg, Blu. *On Women and Judaism: A View from Tradition*. Philadelphia: Jewish Publication Society, 1981.

Jeansonne, Sharon Pace. *The Women of Genesis*. Minneapolis, MN: Fortress Press, 1990.

Harding, M. Esther. *Woman's Mysteries*. New York: G. Putnam's Sons, 1971.

Kaplan, Aryeh. *Waters of Eden: The Mystery of the Mikveh*. New York: NCSY/Union of Orthodox Jewish Congregations, 1976.

King, Ursula. "Goddesses, Witches, Androgyny and Beyond: Feminism and the Transformation of Religious Consciousness." *Women in the World's Religions*. New York: Paragon House, 1987.

Klem, Yonah. "No Ordinary Bath: The Use of the Mikveh in Healing from Incest." *Jewish Women Speak Out: Expanding the Boundaries of Psychology*. Kayla Weiner and Arinna Moon, eds. Seattle: Canopy Press, 1995.

Koltun, Elizabeth, ed. *The Jewish Woman*. New York: Schocken Books, 1976.

Koltuv, Barbara Black. *The Book of Lilith*. York Beach, ME: Nicolas-Hays, Inc., 1987.

Lacks, Roslyn. *Women and Judaism: Myth, History and Struggle*. New York: Doubleday and Co., 1980.

Leibowitz, Nehama. *Studies in Vayikra*. Jerusalem: World Zionist Organization, 1980.

Neumann, Erich. *The Great Mother*. Princeton, NJ: Princeton University Press, 1983.

Newsom, Carol A. and Ringe, Sharon H., eds. *The Women's Bible Commentary*. Louisville, KY: Westminster/John Knox Press, 1992.

Orenstein, Debra ed. *Lifecycles, vol. 1: Jewish Women on Life Passages & Personal Milestones*. Woodstock, VT: Jewish Lights Publishing, 1994.

Orenstein, Debra, and Litman, Jane Rachel, eds. *Lifecycles, vol. 2: Jewish Women on Biblical Themes in Contemporary Life*. Woodstock, VT: Jewish Lights Publishing, 1997.

Cynthia Ozick. "Notes toward Finding the Right Question." *On Being a Jewish Feminist*, Susanna Heschel, ed. New York: Schocken Books, 1983.

Pardes, Ilana. *Countertraditions in the Bible*. Cambridge, MA: Harvard University Press, 1992.

Peskowitz, Miriam and Levitt, Laura, eds. *Judaism Since Gender*. New York: Routledge, 1997.

Phillips, J.A. *Eve: The History of an Idea*. San Francisco: Harper and Row, 1984.

Plaskow, Judith. *Standing Again at Sinai*. San Francisco: Harper San Francisco, 1990.

Plaskow, Judith. "Facing the Ambiguity of God." *Tikkun*, vol. 6, no. 5.

Plaskow, Judith, and Christ, Carole. *Weaving the Visions: New Patterns in Feminist Spirituality*. San Francisco: HarperCollins, 1989.

Plaut, Gunther, ed. *The Torah: A Modern Commentary*. New York: UAHC Press, 1981.

Rosen, Norma. *Biblical Women Unbound*. Philadelphia: Jewish Publication Society, 1996.

Roundtable discussion, "If God Is God She Is Not Nice." *Journal of Feminist Studies in Religion*, vol. 5, no. 1, Spring 1989.

Sarna, Nahum M. *Understanding Genesis*. New York: Schocken Books, 1970.

Sarna, Nahum M. *Exploring Exodus*. New York: Schocken Books, 1987.

Sarna, Nahum M. General editor, *The JPS Torah Commentary*. Philadelphia: Jewish Publication Society, 1991.

Stone, Merlin. *When God Was a Woman*. New York: Dial Press, 1976.

Tolbert, Mary Ann. "Defining the Problem: The Bible and Feminist Hermeneutics." *Semeia*, vol. 28, 1983.

Trible, Phyllis. *Texts of Terror: Literary-Feminist Readings of Biblical Narratives*. Philadelphia: Fortress Press, 1984.

Umansky, Ellen, and Diane Ashton, eds. *Four Centuries of Jewish Women's Spirituality: A Sourcebook*. Boston: Beacon Press, 1992.

Weaver, Mary Jo. "Who Is the Goddess and Where Does She Get Us?" and "Can a Sexist Model Liberate Us? Ancient Near Eastern 'Fertility' Goddesses." *Journal of Feminist Studies in Religion*, vol. 5, no. 1, Spring 1989.

Zones, Jane Sprague, ed. *Taking the Fruit: Modern Women's Tales of the Bible*. Chico, CA: Women's Institute for Continuing Jewish Education, 1981.

Zornberg, Aviva. *Genesis: The Beginning of Desire*. Philadelphia: Jewish Publication Society, 1995.

Index

HUMCA 221
.6082
G624